T0131781

ARE YOU SUPERSTITIOUS?

How A Little Luck Can Change Your Life

TONI KLEIN

ARE YOU SUPERSTITIOUS?
HOW A LITTLE LUCK CAN CHANGE YOUR LIFE

iUniverse books may be ordered through booksellers or by contacting:

iUniverse
1663 Liberty Drive
Bloomington, IN 47403
www.iuniverse.com
1-800-Authors (1-800-288-4677)

ISBN: 978-1-5320-8563-5 (sc)
ISBN: 978-1-5320-8562-8 (e)

Library of Congress Control Number: 2019916918

Print information available on the last page.

iUniverse rev. date: 10/30/2019

To my mother, Rowena, and my departed grandmother, Nell. Thank you for sharing your vast knowledge of superstition and making this book possible.

A special mention to my brother Gustav, my tireless proofreader.

CONTENTS

PREFACE

The subject of superstition is a timeless one, and it has always fascinated me. When I was a small child, my mother, Rowena, began sharing with me her vast knowledge of superstition. Each day, she'd notice an occurrence that related to an aspect of this mysterious subject. For instance, if a black cat crossed our path or salt would spill, she would cite the relevant superstition and the reasoning behind it. I'd eagerly await each new explanation, which gave my mother the opportunity to educate me. As an eager student, I soaked up the information like a sponge.

Rowena had been taught by her mother, my grandmother Nell. Although born in Scotland, Nell had lived in Ireland as a little girl and then relocated to the United States when she was ten years old. She and her mother, my great-grandmother, were psychically inclined. They experienced visionary dreams, witnessed ghosts, and, yes, were highly superstitious. Since my grandmother also talked about superstition, I looked forward to the times she would visit us, when I could enjoy a double-dose of superstitious fun.

I've been interested in writing a book on the topic of superstition for quite a while. As I was penning my last book, *Fairies*, I decided it would be my next venture. Once I arrived at this determination, I had a strange experience while visiting my mother, who inherited the psychic gift from her mother's side of the family. She still lives in my childhood home, and she greeted me with an old notebook, insisting I would need it. I gazed at her quizzically, as I hadn't mentioned my idea of writing about superstition to her yet. At the same time, I became slightly nervous, thinking, *Is this my old secret diary?* Thankfully, it wasn't. However, there it was—my old notepad full of all of the wonderful superstitions I had journaled all those years ago that my mother and grandmother had communicated to me over the years.

Skimming through it, I saw that I had kept a rather detailed account of the very cute scenarios and explanations of the numerous beliefs my mother and grandmother had shared with me. When my Grandmother Nell would visit, she'd stay with us at least a week or two every few months. I adored this time with Nell, especially when she shared superstitions with me, which was at least twice a day. It was so interesting when she and my mother would naturally launch into a story or explanation of a superstition when a certain word, phrase, or discussion spurred it. It was a bonus when Nell built onto my mother's version, which added to the explanation rather nicely.

As I was growing up—and to this day—I enjoyed the mystery and unknown aspects that life offered. After school each day, my older sisters and I would race to the television to watch the popular serial, *Dark Shadows*. Even though I was very young, I sat beside them on the floor, cross-legged, very close to the TV screen, to engage in the eerie scenarios. I wasn't frightened but mesmerized. We all loved the plot and the enchanting characters, especially Barnabas Collins.

Other television shows we had to watch were *The Sixth Sense*, a paranormal series starring Gary Collins, and *Night Gallery*, hosted by Rod Serling. Looking back, I was probably too young to watch such programs, but I really enjoyed them.

My childhood patterns led me to be the person I am today—one who loves superstition and the world it surrounds. I was raised on it, and it was all around me. I feel that when things seem uncanny, the world in which we live becomes so much more interesting!

INTRODUCTION

Welcome to the intriguing world of superstition. Kudos to you! By selecting *Are You Superstitious? How a Little Luck Can Change Your Life*, you have demonstrated that you are an open-minded individual who will give the world of superstition a chance. Furthermore, you are an individual who is not locked into subscribing only to the world in scientific terms, but in a mysterious sense as well.

Prepare to be entertained and intrigued by the many superstitions in this world. You'll learn the origins of both common and not-so-common superstitions. You'll see why some customs are so entrenched in our belief systems that they become second nature. I'll explain why superstitions are currently followed in our advanced society, even though the reason why they began may not fit into the contemporary world. You'll gain knowledge on the background of superstitions and why they have been carried through the ages into the present day. You'll see who is more superstitious by gender and why the time period or country in which you were born could matter. I'll explain why certain numbers are so important or scary to us. Plus, I hope you'll be charmed by the lyrics and meanings of songs written and/ or sung by famous music personalities who have superstitious natures and have shared their feelings through their music.

In addition, five journal pages have been placed at the end of this book so you can write notes.

As you read the explanations of how and why certain superstitions have come about and why people have followed the practices through time, you may decide to follow these superstitions until you leave this earth, or you may decide to toss one or two out the window. For instance, as you will see in a later chapter, the superstitious response of throwing salt over one's shoulder, which many people do still practice today, does not quite stand up in today's society.

Provided below is a brief chapter-by-chapter overview:

Chapter 1—What Is a Superstition?
Superstition is explained. An overview is given of the percentage of American believers, and the views of superstitious versus nonsuperstitious individuals are discussed. The difference between superstition and symbolism is explained.

Chapter 2—The Mystique of the Black Cat
The black cat is one of the most recognized superstitions. We will delve into the reasons why the black cat stands out more than any other color, as well as the history of this feline.

Chapter 3—Friday the Thirteenth and the Number Thirteen
This chapter highlights the highly feared date and number thirteen. *Paraskevidekatriaphobia* and *Triskaidekaphobia* are explained, as well as why otherwise rational individuals experience anxiety over this number and date, and other facts that will surely send shivers down your spine.

Chapter 4—Wedding Superstitions
A look at how such a happy time is surrounded with many beliefs, good and bad. Let the bride beware!

Chapter 5—The Evil Eye
Learn how a mere glare may ruin your day and what protection is available to ward off the dangerous evil eye.

Chapter 6—Birds and Superstition
This chapter offers insight into a variety of birds and how they relate to superstition. Understand their mysterious and powerful nature and which birds are considered lucky and unlucky.

Chapter 7—Superstitions Surrounding the Canine and the Feline
The superstitious differences between the dog and the cat are examined. How many cats and dogs live with us in the United States? What does a howling dog foretell, and why are cats believed to have nine lives? Travel through time and read about the beginning of cat history and why they were so revered, then persecuted and hunted, and finally appreciated once again.

Chapter 8—Gemstones and Superstition
Which gemstones offer protection, and which deal bad luck? Explore the world of lucky and unlucky gemstones.

Chapter 9—Lucky Superstitions Practiced to Bring Good Luck
A collection of feel-good superstitions is featured. You will read about the origin and representations of several lucky charms, including the horseshoe, the wishbone, amulets, the four-leaf clover, pennies, and much more.

Chapter 10—Superstitions Practiced to Prevent Bad Luck
A review of numerous unlucky beliefs is featured. Is there a legitimate reason why the number thirteen should be considered unlucky? Why are black cats viewed as scary and unlucky? Will finding a four-leaf clover bring good fortune? If a rabbit's foot is lucky, wouldn't the original owner (that is, the rabbit) still own it? Even though we may believe that rational thinking is beside the point when it comes to unlucky superstitions, these beliefs are so ingrained in our culture and our minds that critical thinking may be the best way to beat our obsession with them.

Chapter 11—Superstition: Men versus Women
Take a journey and explore the very different perspectives and stances that males and females take toward superstition. I highlight a study I conducted.

Appendix 1—Thirteen Tales of Superstition
Dive into this assembly of true accounts according to sources from different backgrounds and age groups.

Appendix 2—Thirteen Songs of Superstition
Enjoy lyrics and my personal assessment of thirteen tunes by famous musical artists.

It was my pleasure to compile this distinctive guide. By the time you've finished reading this book, I hope you will be able to astonish your friends and family with the knowledge you have gained from reading it. You will be the interesting spark required at any mingle event.

I am happy to have a belief in the unknown, and I hope many others subscribe to this philosophy and give the realm of superstition a chance.

Everything has a place on this earth, and superstition is no different. For now, sit back, relax, and be entertained. Consider yourself in good hands with the savant of superstition.

Chapter 1

WHAT IS SUPERSTITION?

Superstition is the poetry of life.

—Johann Wolfgang von Goethe

What is superstition? Is it an illogical thought? Is it an immature notion shared among children? As the expression goes, "Step on a crack, you'll break your mother's back." When I was young, I took that expression seriously and tried to avoid cracks in the pavement as best as I could, although I noticed most of the boys on the playground did not. *Merriam-Webster* defines *superstition* as "a belief or practice resulting from ignorance, fear of the unknown, trust in magic or chance, or a false conception of causation"; *superstitious* is defined as "of, relating to, or swayed by a superstition." Common synonyms for superstition include fallacy, delusion, misconception, fantasy, or false notion. (Who can really declare the unknown is false?)

Are you superstitious? In an article by Gallup.com, "One in Four Americans Superstitious" (2000), David W. Moore reported,

> In a September 1996 Gallop poll, 25% of Americans acknowledged that they were "very" (1%) or "somewhat" (24%) superstitious, up from 18% who said that in 1990. The poll also shows that younger people tend to be more superstitious that older people. Over a third (35%) of those

1

under the age of 30 said they were superstitious, but the
percentage declines as people get older, so that only 17%
of those 65 and older were superstitious.

Common superstitions included believing it was bad luck to walk under a
ladder, to break a mirror, or to have a black cat cross one's path. Personally,
I'm surprised that, according to Moore's article, the younger generation
polled as being more superstitious than the older folks.

Superstition exists in every culture, whether based on personal beliefs,
myths, old wives' tales, or traditions communicated through folklore.
Because superstitions are often passed down through word of mouth over
the years, it is possible that anything may have been "lost in translation."
Superstitions, whether entertaining or eerie, are woven into the fabric of
life.

Generally, superstition tends to be arbitrary, as it may center around an
object (such as a mirror or a penny), an animal (the infamous black cat
or a rabbit's foot), a date (Friday the thirteenth), the deceased (placing
a personal item in the coffin so the dead may claim it in the afterlife), or
graveyards (placing flowers or gifts on the grave to make the spirit happy).
A person might consider a particular superstition comforting because it
serves as a form of protection by warding off evil or by eliciting good
luck. A superstition may belong to a certain culture, group, or tradition,
or simply be unique to an individual and have no bearing on society or
religion. For instance, a student may use his or her lucky pen during an
exam to score a high grade, or a sports player may turn his or her socks
inside out before every game for good luck.

Superstitions exist all over the globe. Some trace back to the Middle Ages,
while others go even further back to ancient Egyptian times. Even though
the Western world considers itself a scientific society, it shares in many
superstitious beliefs, as does the rest of the world.

I enjoy superstitions that stem from all walks of life. It appears that all
cultures have at least one superstitious practice. For example, in the Jewish
culture, if something is considered evil, a person says "Pooh, pooh, pooh",
which then gives that person a shield against negative forces. Over time, this

expression replaced the act of spitting three times, as that was considered an unsightly practice.

How do the nonsuperstitious feel toward the superstitious? It apparently is not a positive view. I have spoken to disbelievers who claim others use the guise of being superstitious to attribute their misfortune to bad luck. Disbelievers also view the superstitious ones as playing a blame game, instead of thinking they contributed to the situation. This approach is likely easier and more comforting than admitting mistakes. Thus, to blame bad luck is less stressful than to admit personal defeat. Furthermore, individuals who try to control situations through lucky items or traditions are more likely to slant luck in their own favor by wearing certain amulets, carrying a rabbit's foot, performing rituals, and the like.

For some, it is difficult to fathom that anyone would choose to believe in an invisible, unmeasurable force over his or her own agency. Yet I have noticed that even those who claim they are *not* superstitious will blow out birthday candles, dodge a black cat, avoid a ladder, or say "God bless you" after someone sneezes. My personal thought is, Why not ensure some good luck, if we can?

Although some Americans act as if the concept of luck is silly, throughout history, folks have altered their lives to accommodate superstitious beliefs.

Who is superstitious? Interestingly, various presidents of the United States seem to have had a superstitious nature. According to Mandi Kerr's article, "The Strange Superstitions of American Presidents, Revealed" (2019), presidents Barack Obama and Ronald Reagan believed in good luck charms. Harry Truman placed a lucky horseshoe over his door in the White House. Franklin Roosevelt feared the number thirteen. Other presidents felt or saw ghostly presences in the White House, and one even witnessed UFO activity (although not at the White House). Donald Trump throws salt over his shoulder and is known to be highly superstitious. The reason he throws salt over his shoulder—not when it's spilled but after each meal—is said to be because if the devil is prowling about, he will not cause distraction or harm.

It is comforting to know those who run our government are often as cautious as I am and believe as much as I do.

Superstition versus Symbolism
Superstition and symbolism are quite different, yet one may think otherwise. Let's review the meaning of superstition: "a belief or practice resulting from ignorance, fear of the unknown, trust in magic or chance, or a false conception of causation."

What is symbolism? According to *Merriam-Webster*, it is

> 1: the art or practice of using symbols especially by investing things with a symbolic meaning or by expressing the invisible or intangible by means of visible or sensuous representations: such as
>> a: artistic imitation or invention that is a method of revealing or suggesting immaterial, ideal, or otherwise intangible truth or states
>> b: the use of conventional or traditional signs in the representation of divine beings and spirits
> 2: a system of symbols or representations

Basically, superstition seems connected with illogical thoughts, whereas symbolism is dependent on logic. Even though, on some level, a mysterious, supernatural correlation exists between superstition and symbolism, the definition of superstition seems rather harsh. It portrays superstition as serving the ill-informed, visionless masses who heartily accept certain notions without authentication, while keeping society fear-based. On the other hand, symbolism is reasonable; it's open to interpretation, reassurance, and greater meaning through a spiritual link. For instance, noticing a cardinal symbolically represents that a positive event will occur in your life or that a deceased relative or friend is saying hello. Biblically, the bird's red color is a symbol of the blood and everlasting love of Christ. Yet superstition says that spotting a blackbird on a roof or chimney foretells a death, and there is no room for analysis. Symbolically, birds, in general, forecast clear vision, guardianship, and a happy prospect for the future.

I have my own definitions of superstition and symbolism:

Superstition: an absolute warning of a bad omen or good luck to come. It is a series of beliefs passed down through time, societies, and families. It does not represent a portrayal to only an ignorant group or person.

Symbolism: a sign that is specific to one individual that provides him or her the opportunity to decipher its special meaning, based on current circumstances. For instance, I recently lost someone very special in my life. As I was speaking about this person to my mother, I gazed out the window and noticed a beautiful cardinal perch for a moment and then fly away. Because I knew what the bird represented, I perceived that special being was sending a hello expressly to me.

Superstition is definitely in the land of the unknown. For as long as there have been folklore, old wives' tales, or scary happenings, superstition has influenced civilizations across the globe. Certainly, we cannot escape superstition, because every group has its fair share. I believe that most superstitions obliterate rational thought processes, even though the world has become more educated and modernized.

On a positive note, superstition may serve as a welcome diversion and offer a level of solace, with the thought that good luck may be around the corner. Superstition, however, is discredited by the naysayers, who interpret it as false and unscientific. Yet I know better! There are just some things in life that we cannot logically explain.

Superstition is the need to view the world in
terms of simple cause and effect.
—Bernard Beckett

Chapter 2

THE MYSTIQUE OF
THE BLACK CAT

A black cat crossing your path signifies that
the animal is going somewhere.

—Groucho Marx

I love cats, and to me, all colors are adorable. Superstitions involving the mystique of the black cat are woven into American history. To most, the black cat has a wicked reputation. It's looked upon suspiciously, but in an odd sense, it's respected more than cats of other colors because of the power it may carry. The feline sporting this particular hue carries a mystical role that cats of other colors do not have, and it is assigned sinister qualities. Over time, cats, with their keen senses and agile movements, became associated with witches, Halloween, evil, bad luck, and an overall sense of eeriness. The media and folktales have great influence on the way black cats are viewed. A few superstitions are immediately associated with bad luck, and the black cat is unquestionably one of them.

The following superstitions are associated with black cats:

Black Cat That Crosses Your Path

One of the more popular superstitions about black cats is that it's bad luck if one crosses your path, but what does this really indicate? Is it really more dangerous to see a black cat walk in front of you than to see a car suddenly appear out of nowhere? Perhaps. What are the advantages of keeping a black cat out of your path? My grandmother alleged that in some European countries, folks believe that death would occur shortly after the black "moggy" darted in front of you. Yet in Ireland and Germany, the black cat may be considered lucky. For instance, if a black cat crosses your path from left to right, it is a *good* omen. Here in the United States, we tend to believe that black cats that cross our paths create general misfortune. There seem to be an inordinate number of black kitties in the small city in which I reside, so I prefer the good-luck philosophy.

Witches and Black Cats

Many old wives' tales explain that black cats are connected to witches. Hence, if a black cat crosses your path, it is assumed that the negativity from the witch is passed to the individual. Legend tells that a witch is able to transform herself into a black cat in order to trick people or that a black cat may act as an assistant to the sorceress. The witch's goal is to change into the cat to mysteriously prance in the shadows, casting spells on unsuspecting individuals. This was a popular thought in Salem, Massachusetts, during the witch trial era. Merely being a female and owning a black cat would deem the unfortunate woman as a witch, and she was sentenced to death.

Today, Salem remains steeped in urban myths, especially so during the Halloween season. I have visited Salem in October, and it is quite entertaining. I recommend it.

As I mentioned, there seem to be quite a few black cats in my neighborhood, and they often cross my path. I remind myself, however, that for the superstition to hold true, the cat has to be a *completely* black cat. Surely, I reason, there is a tiny patch of color on its fur somewhere.

Black Cats throughout History

Black cats were not always a sign of evil; in fact, they were regarded very highly. In ancient Egypt, black cats were worshipped, and killing one was punishable by death. The Egyptians realized cats were worthwhile creatures, as they protected food stocks from rats, mice, and other critters that caused disease. In that era, families mourned the death of their cats as if family members had passed. Moreover, it was popular for cat owners and their cats to be buried together, or they would choose to mummify the cats after death. Bastet, part cat and part woman, was the Egyptian goddess who granted good fortune to those who sheltered and protected cats.

Fortunately, not all tales of the black cat are ominous. When I was a little girl, my grandmother related a legend of a female black cat. I love cats, so I asked her every time she visited to tell this story to me, and she patiently obliged. Here it is: In ancient Egypt, there was a goddess who was a black cat, and her name was Bastet. She was a very kind cat who wanted to ensure all good people made it straight to heaven after they died. Bastet knew that sometimes diabolical souls would try to block souls from entering heaven. Hence, Bastet created a divine barrier against any evil souls to ensure that good people arrived without incident.

There are other stories about the cat goddess, but I enjoyed my grandmother's version.

By the Middle Ages, black cats were no longer revered because it was believed they were connected to unseemly older women who practiced black magic. As the news spread about the black cat, mass slaughtering took place. In the UK, black cats were seen in a positive light, but unfortunately, they often were mistreated and misunderstood. In the 1600s, the Pilgrims felt that a black cat represented evil and the devil.

In Japan, cats generally carry a positive meaning, symbolizing good fortune and prosperity, including black cats. You might have seen a Maneki-Neko, a common Japanese cat figurine, when shopping or dining out. Some businesses display a Maneki-Neko posed with one paw up, as if beckoning to draw in good fortune.

Interestingly, single women in Japan sometimes own a black cat because it's believed the cat will attract many suitors.

Black Cats—More Unlikely to Be Adopted
Currently in the United States, many people think the black cat is unlucky; some folks have been conditioned to view the black cat as a mark of bad luck. Black cats are not a popular choice at shelters. An article on Weird News, "Black Cats Less than Half as Likely to Be Adopted as Gray Cats" (2017), noted that black cats have more difficulty in receiving a home. For this reason, shelters sometimes offer incentives, such as free spaying or neutering or a discount on the price of adoption, in order for the black cats to receive a home. Apparently, this superstition is still a very strong one.

However, this superstition was not followed by my sister, Megan, or by my niece, Tess. They adopted a beautiful black cat named Raven. Raven is adored and rocks their house!

Black Cat Theories

- Black cats are associated with evil, and they suck the life from babies.
- In Scotland, if an unknown black cat arrives at your door, it's believed that money also will arrive.
- In Italy, to hear a black cat sneeze indicates a splash of good luck is on the way.
- If you attend a wedding in Northamptonshire, Derbyshire, or Nottinghamshire, England, feel free to give a black cat as a wedding gift. It is well received and thought of as a good omen.
- In the Netherlands, black cats are not allowed in the room when the family is discussing financial matters since this may cause a monetary loss.
- The Irish believe a person who kills a black cat will receive seven years bad luck.
- In the Old South of the United States, any black kitty who enters the room during a private family discussion will spread the gossip all over town.
- Sailors are not fond of black cats. If one walks on board but leaves suddenly, the ship is doomed. In the olden days, pirates were wary

if a black cat approached them; it was felt that death would be upon them during the next voyage.

- The women in the sailors' families had a different outlook. Seamen's wives felt that having a black cat as a pet would ensure their husbands' safe journey home from the sea. Also, it was extra lucky to bring the cat along to greet any arriving ships that carried loved ones.
- The Japanese culture considers black cats as guardians of ill children and protectors who won't let evil into the home.

Society has now evolved to the point that black cats are no longer hunted or linked to black magic. Cat lovers can attest that all cats are lovable, no matter the hue, and they bring years of happiness and enjoyment. Let's learn from the quote by Groucho Marx at the beginning of this chapter. It is very reasonable and straightforward. Basically, when a black cat crosses your path, it is crossing; nothing more, nothing less. In fact, the cat, a highly independent being, is crossing because it has a mission, and most likely, we are not part of its mission.

If you believe a black cat is bad luck, people think you're crazy, but plenty of times, if I see a black cat down my street, I turn around and go the other way. Even if I'm late. I'll be late for the airport and be in a limo, and if I see a black cat, I'll be like, "Sir, you have to turn around and go down the next street."

—Missy Elliott

Chapter 3

FRIDAY THE THIRTEENTH AND THE NUMBER THIRTEEN

I've always regarded my Monday the thirteenth
as people do their Friday the thirteenth.

—Toni Klein

Simply said, Friday the thirteenth and the number thirteen are viewed as bad luck. In this chapter, we will explore the date that panics the dickens out of many folks, as well as exploring the number thirteen. The mere mention of this number or knowing a month has a Friday the thirteenth in it may cause some people to cringe and feel stressed.

Friday the Thirteenth

Let's place the number thirteen and Friday together—what a combination! This date has generated shudders up and down spines for centuries. Why are people so apprehensive? How did you feel when you hear or read the words, Friday or thirteen?

Friday the thirteenth is a terrifying day to many individuals. In Laura Mitchell's article, "Is it *really* dangerous to fly on Friday the thirteenth? The truth will shock you" (2018), she states, "[Seventy-two percent] of people claim to have experienced bad luck on Friday the thirteenth, flight prices are cut and many flyers will not travel during the 24-hour period." Ms. Mitchell proves that it is actually safer to travel on Friday the thirteenth: "The average number of fatal aircraft crashes on Friday the 13th days is 0.067 per day, compared to a usual average of 0.091, according to a statistical analysis by the Aviation Safety Network, conducted in 2013."

By itself, Friday intimidates some folks all by itself. My mother professed to never buy a car on a Friday or start any a new project. I never questioned that; I willingly accepted the information as gospel truth, as we do with so many of superstitions. According to legend, the following events fell on a Friday: Jesus was crucified, and Adam and Eve were driven from the garden of Eden. The early Brits reserved Fridays for public hangings, and the ancient Romans held their executions on Fridays. It is no wonder that Friday, coupled with the thirteenth day of the month, is considered so unlucky. When we combine a day that people perceive as unfortunate with the number thirteen—also considered unlucky—it can be disastrous.

As I was writing this book, my brother, Gustav, and I were discussing the superstitions from our youth. He reminded me of two key terms. One, a combination of the Greek words for Friday and the number thirteen, *paraskevidekatriaphobia*, is the fear of Friday the thirteenth. The second term, *triskaidekaphobia*, is the fear of the number thirteen. My mother, a former English teacher, would impart a variety of information to us children and had mentioned these words to us. I will augment our vocabulary lesson with one more term—*hippopotomonstrosesquippedaliophobia*, the fear of long words. Children's songwriter Bryant Oden wrote "The Long Word Song" (2011). He sings that lengthy word while instructing how to enunciate it. You can find his songs on YouTube.

How did Friday the thirteenth get its reputation? It was a culmination of events that finally resulted in anxiety over time, which then evolved into a large-scale panic. During the medieval era, the Knights Templar, who were virtuous Catholics, formed a powerful yet secretive and rather large society. The Knights Templar were a military army who did not operate under the chosen regime of the time. Their goal was to protect the voyagers who took pilgrimages to particular unchartered locations in the Holy Land. They also carried out military missions. Although considered a very powerful and strong group, they were captured and ultimately arrested. The king of France alleged heresy, and later, the group disbanded. Folklore reports that their imprisonment and the beginning of the horrible torture inflicted upon this association occurred on Friday the thirteenth.

Sailors feel that Fridays and the thirteenth of the month and certainly the combination of the two are an especially unlucky time to launch a ship. Folklore relates that in the eighteenth century, a high-profile ship commanded by Captain Friday was set to sail on a Friday the thirteenth. It never returned to port. At that juncture, seamen considered the thirteenth and Friday taboo. Perhaps architects, builders, and sailors are just a little superstitious.

Novelists and horror-movie writers have popularized the evilness of Friday the thirteenth. One example is the novel by Thomas W. Lawson, *Friday, the Thirteenth*. On film, the series of *Friday the 13th* movies was quite popular. I saw a total of seven of those movies and also loved the television series, *Friday the 13th*. This series featured an antique store, and in each episode, the staff at the store recovered cursed antiques and then locked them in a vault for safekeeping. This program lasted three seasons, which was not long enough, in my opinion. Let's hope they recovered all of the evil objects.

It can be heartbreaking for those who experience paraskevidekatriaphobia. The following are possible symptoms:

- a shortness of breath, wheezing, gasping for air, or feeling faint
- chest pains or a heart-attack sensation
- a sense of panic
- breaking down in tears or nervous laughter
- shakiness
- a fear of going to work or ceasing normal responsibilities on that date

Paraskevidekatriaphobia may be a serious condition for some individuals. Those who feel the symptoms described above should consider seeking professional help. Trained therapists or medical doctors may offer relief, or you may choose to read books on phobias. My brother Gustav recalled reading of a treatment center in Nevada specifically designed for treating paraskevidekatriaphobia. It's comforting to know help is available for those who need it.

My sister Megan and I agree that we have more trepidation when a Monday the thirteenth approaches than a Friday the thirteenth. Our Fridays are fine, but our Mondays are usually fraught with angst. Personally, I believe that Mondays should receive the same bad reputation. Typically, adults do not look forward to going to work on Mondays, and children dread returning to school after the weekend.

Listed below are a few celebrities who were born on Friday the thirteenth:

- Peter Tork (musician, the Monkees)
- Mary-Kate and Ashley Olsen (actresses, *Full House*)
- Julia Louis-Dreyfus (actress, *Seinfeld*)
- Tony Dow (actor, *Leave it to Beaver*)
- Frances Conroy (actress, *American Horror Story*).
- Didi Conn (actress, *Grease*)
- Max Weinberg (drummer, E Street Band)
- Christopher Plummer (film actor)
- Kate Walsh (actress, *Grey's Anatomy*)

According to Stephanie Pappas's article "13 Freaky Things That Happened on Friday the 13th" (2015), thirteen bizarre events have occurred over time on Friday the thirteenth. A summarization of her findings is listed below.

1. A daredevil's death leap

On a Friday the thirteenth in the 1800s, while performing a stunt, daredevil Sam Patch leapt to his death into the Genesee River in New York.

2. The "Black Friday" fires

In Australia, on Friday, January 13, 1939, a terrible fire claimed the lives of many people.

3. Buckingham Palace bombed

In September 1940, while King George VI and Queen Elizabeth were at tea, the Nazis bombed the palace. This was one of many bombings, yet this particular one took place on Friday the thirteenth. The good news is that the palace sustained only minimal damage.

4. Kansas floods

In 1951, the water level of the Kansas River rose to sixteen inches after nonstop rain for five straight days. On Friday, July 13, the river rose to a record high, reaching 40.8 feet. This caused much destruction to the Midwest and its surrounding area, as it was horribly flooded. Individuals were forced to relocate and others passed away due to the flood.

5. A Cold War crisis

In 1952, a Swedish military aircraft was shot down by the Soviet Union on Friday, June 13. Eight individuals from that plane perished. Of those eight, four were discovered on the bottom of the Baltic Sea, while the four other crew members were never recovered. The wreckage of the plane is exhibited at the Swedish Air Force Museum.

6. A murder goes ignored

In the Big Apple, New York City, on Friday, March 13, 1964, a heinous murder took place. A female bar manager, Kitty Genovese, was brutally stabbed and physically ravaged for over thirty minutes while, oddly, eye-witnesses did nothing to stop or report the act. Later, this murder led to a popular psychology theory taught in college classes, titled the "bystander effect" or "Kitty Genovese syndrome."

7. A deadly cyclone strikes

A tropical storm hit Bangladesh on Friday, November 13, 1970, killing several hundred thousand people. It was classified as a category 3 hurricane. The water surge pushed up to sixteen feet, and the natives had little chance to evacuate. The ones who did survive were mainly males who were strong enough to climb high trees and who had the muscle to cling to the trees until the storm subsided. The very young, elderly, and sickly females perished.

8. An infamous story of survival begins

On Friday, October 13, 1972, a plane with forty-five passengers bound for Chili crashed into a mountain peak. Initially, there were twenty-seven survivors. Unfortunately, some passed away due to starvation (even though they ate the dead in an effort to survive short-term), an avalanche, and frigid weather conditions. Later, two of the passengers decided to hike out on a mission to reach help. Due to their brave effort, nearly two months after the crash, sixteen people were rescued on December 23. This is truly amazing, and the passengers were so very courageous.

9. A lesser-known plane crash kills 174

On Friday, October 13, 1972 (the same date as number 8, above), a plane flying from Paris to Moscow crashed while trying to land at a scheduled stop in Leningrad. It was reported to have hit the ground with such great force that everyone aboard was killed instantly. The cause of the crash was never determined.

10. Tupac Shakur dies

On Friday, September 13, 1996, rapper Tupac Shakur passed away from gunshot wounds he'd received a few days earlier in Las Vegas. Theories for the shooting range from gangs, to feuds, to business dealings. Conspiracy theories exist that state that Tupac did not actually die. Such theories exist for Elvis Presley as well.

11. A master of suspense turns one hundred

It is only fitting that the king of suspense, Alfred Hitchcock, was born on such an eerie date—August 13, 1899—although he wasn't born on a Friday. If he had lived to see his one hundredth birthday, he would have celebrated on the scary date: Friday the thirteenth. Personally, I admire Hitchcock's work and cannot decide which thriller I love more, *Psycho* or *The Birds*.

12. Freak blizzard hits Buffalo

Buffalo, New York, suffered a blizzard on Friday, October 13, 2006. Inhabitants of Buffalo, who are accustomed to a great deal of snowfall, did not expect such an accumulation, which totaled twenty-two inches on that day and produced a major power outage that lasted for days. It affected nearly one million people in the Buffalo region. How very bizarre that this blizzard took place in the autumn month of October. However, anything is possible when an event occurs on a Friday and is coupled with the number thirteen.

13. A cruise ship capsizes

The last and most recent Friday-the-thirteenth catastrophe concerns a cruise ship that hit a reef off the Isola del Giglio, an Italian island. As a result of the impact, the ship began to tip and eventually it rested on its side. The date was Friday, January 13, 2012. Some survivors jumped into lifeboats, while others were airlifted to safety. Despite rescue efforts, thirty-two people died in this incident.

What message did these thirteen grisly accounts convey to you? Are you now convinced that Friday the thirteenth is unlucky? According to the Gregorian calendar, we encounter a Friday the thirteenth at least once a year, sometimes two or even three a year. Perhaps a good piece of advice is to carry a lucky amulet when traveling.

The Number Thirteen

People in the United States usually think *oh no* concerning the number thirteen. How would you feel if your hotel room was number thirteen or if your office or apartment was located on the thirteenth floor? Better yet, what if the number of your brand-new house was thirteen? If you claim to be unaffected by it, you would be considered the exception. My guess is that most of us would feel at least a twinge of trepidation. Certainly, most people would rather be associated with any other number than thirteen (except possibly 666). Plausible reasons exist why, throughout time, the human race has been conditioned to feel this way about the number. What follows are some of the more popular explanations.

One reason the number thirteen has been linked to bad luck comes from the early Norse and Christians. The Scandinavians alleged that the number thirteen was not a lucky omen because they thought that twelve mythological gods assisted their lives in a positive way. Yet later in time, an evil thirteenth did join the twelve and from that time laid misfortune upon man.

A second speculation on why thirteen is considered taboo returns to the period of the Last Supper. Jesus seated thirteen at his Last Supper table, the thirteenth guest being Judas. Judas was a traitor who was paid thirty pieces of silver to identify Jesus to the Roman authorities. He accepted this price and betrayed Jesus, who was later captured by Pontus Pilate's soldiers. The next day, Jesus was put to death on the cross. Today, it is not advisable to place thirteen individuals at a table, for fear a death will occur within a year's time.

Last year, I attended a dinner party. The hostess secretly communicated to me that she had placed fourteen around the table, yet one person had suddenly canceled. She became frightened at the thought of sitting around a table of thirteen. After I agreed that I did not feel comfortable myself, we formulated a plan that we were sure would counteract any possible ill effects: we placed a doll in the empty seat. The others thought it was a lark, but we knew the real reason behind the doll and chuckled.

In France, highly superstitious people will hire extra dinner guests in an effort to avoid thirteen at the table. Former President Teddy Roosevelt refused to be seated at a table with only thirteen guests; he also would not travel on the thirteenth of any month.

A third root that gives people pause and connects the number thirteen with bad luck is the gallows. Centuries ago, when a criminal was sentenced to death, he or she were required to walk to the gallows, and it took thirteen steps to get there.

Numerologists consider that thirteen is a wicked number. They suggest the number twelve is the ultimate, perfect number. Hence, the next number in line throws the scheme out of whack. Moreover, there are twelve zodiac signs and twelve months in the calendar year; thus, more proof that thirteen is deemed unlucky and apparently unwanted.

Hotels and other tall buildings have been known to skip the thirteenth floor by numbering the floor after the twelfth as the fourteenth floor. Certain housing developments do not have house addresses with a number thirteen. Some hospitals avoid a room thirteen. A few airlines elect to skip the thirteenth aisle.

Geography may play into the various beliefs concerning numbers and luck. A friend, Cenzina, whose family originates in Italy, related that the number thirteen is considered quite lucky in that country. She explained there is an expression, *fare tredici*, which translates as "to do thirteen." *Fare tredici* indicates hitting the jackpot. In Italy, the unlucky number is seventeen, and it's disliked in the way thirteen is in the United States. Belgium also considers thirteen to be a lucky number. Some employees may receive a bonus paycheck called a "thirteenth month," therefore making it a favorable number. Here in the United States, thirteen surely has quite a different meaning.

A 2016 study by Maria De Paola, titled "Gender Differences in Superstition— Men are influenced by good omens, women by the unlucky," reported that over seven hundred Italian students (males and females) were scheduled to take an exam. Their assigned seat numbers were either thirteen, seventeen, or thirty, as well as other random, insignificant numbers. Remember that in Italy, the number thirteen is considered lucky, as is number thirty; seventeen is considered unlucky.

The test proved gender differences with regard to superstition. Based on this study and prior data, researchers found that "women are more fearful than men of potentially negative outcomes and more prone to pessimism."

Thirteen Fun Facts about the Number Thirteen

1. A baker's dozen includes thirteen, not twelve. (My kind of dozen!)

2. The United States had thirteen original colonies.

3. Friday the thirteenth occurs only in a month that begins on a Sunday.

4. Numerologists consider thirteen to be an unlucky number, yet mathematicians refer to it as a very pleasing number.

5. Songstress Taylor Swift apparently adores this number. She was born on December 13 and turned thirteen on a Friday the thirteenth. Ms. Swift is so superstitious that she draws the number thirteen on her hand before every performance for good luck.

6. Scientists do not believe that Friday the thirteenth, the number thirteen, or any superstition of any kind has an effect on us.

7. Alexander the Great wished to be a god. If he had lived, he may have been considered the thirteenth in his time period. When he passed away, however, people began to think of the number thirteen as unlucky.

8. Centuries ago, the noose was used for hanging convicted criminals and fashioned with thirteen wraps above the actual noose.

9. Thirteen is a prime number.

10. In a standard fifty-two–card deck of playing cards, four suits of thirteen exist.

11. The infamous murderers Charles Manson and Jack the Ripper had names with thirteen letters. (Did you count the letters too?)

12. The death card is the thirteenth card in the Tarot deck. (As scary as it sounds, the death card actually foretells a new beginning.)

13. When I was thirteen years old, my parents let me have thirteen cats—we lived on a farm and had plenty of space. Every day after school, all thirteen cats and I would take a long walk together, strolling along in a group. As I look back on this, the cats walking with me is difficult to believe, as cats are very independent. I still miss them and our walks together. We shared a very close bond.

What is the number thirteen after all? On a positive note, it is the number one and three, side by side. The number one is seen as a self-governing number and possesses nothing extraordinary in a negative sense. The number three is a magical number, representing the Trinity. Plus, we all know that a genie grants three wishes. It is always helpful to maintain a positive outlook.

Thanks to our ancestors, friends, television shows, authors, and other types of media, the superstition relating to Friday the thirteenth and the number thirteen will continue to live on in our minds and hearts. Surely this belief will be carried beyond our lifetimes, as well of those of our children.

Sometimes you lose, sometimes you win,
sometimes you are unlucky, but that's life.

—Jerome Boateng

Chapter 4

WEDDING SUPERSTITIONS

Weddings are important because they are about life and possibility.

—Anne Hathaway

Weddings are steeped in tradition and linked to numerous superstitions. Typically, even folks who do not view themselves as particularly superstitious, feel obligated to go with the flow. No one wishes to risk ruining their special day. Since wedding superstitions are so deeply rooted in our society and often enhance the celebration, we automatically comply without a second thought. The act of throwing the bouquet in one example.

A large number of wedding superstitions are available—to enjoy, beware of, or ignore. Typically, the ones that spring to mind generally are related to the wedding day, dress, or rings. This chapter will offer many interesting wedding superstitions, including those on the veil, wedding cake, threshold, wedding day weather, and much more. These various beliefs have different origins and stem from different traditions. Yet whatever their roots, the central theme of this chapter is to not take any chances and ruin your wedding day.

The Popularity of Marriage
Marriage is a popular commodity, which is so many couples feel the need to the follow the superstitions pertaining to it. Statistica.com notes that

in 2017, in the United States, the marriage rate was approximately 60.8 million compared to 1960, more than fifty years earlier, which was 40.2. Although the 2017 amount seems a considerable jump as compared to the year 1960, the rise likely is only a reflection of the overall growth in population.

Location! Location! Location!
Why is Las Vegas, Nevada, a popular place for nuptials? Sin City offers a quick, easy, and cheap way to go. The marriage-license requirements are lenient, and Vegas is lucky! After all, everything in Vegas involves Lady Luck.

The allure of Vegas is mesmerizing and attracts many. According to Nevada state records, 120,000 ceremonies take place each year; that's about three hundred nuptials per day. The most popular wedding date is February 14, or Valentine's Day. Can you guess its runner-up? It is December 31, New Year's Eve. This exciting locale is where Elvis Presley and his fiancée, Priscilla, were married in 1967. They flew into Sin City at 3:00 a.m., secured their license, and were married by 9:00 a.m. Easy-peasy!

The Wedding Dress
The wedding dress is a sacred garment, and myriad superstitions surround it. The dress is a personal reflection of the bride's taste mixed together with her ancestry and, in past times, her family's economic status. In the Western world, brides commonly wear a white dress. This was popularized by Britain's Queen Victoria in the nineteenth century. In centuries past, prosperous families offered their daughters fine fabrics and fancy adornments. Brides who belonged to the poorer classes usually donned their finest church dresses.

What superstitions are connected to the wedding gown? At what point should the bride beware? Many negative beliefs do exist. One awful conception is that the bride must not rip her gown while dressed in it; if she does, the groom will die within a short time. Another notion instructs the bride-to-be to not take part in the sewing of any portion of her wedding dress. Why? Again, a death may result, though not necessarily the groom's.

Most of us are familiar with the tradition that it is unlucky for the groom to see the bride before the wedding? Yes, that still holds true today.

Another note to any superstitious prospective bride: do not try on your entire wedding ensemble (dress, shoes, veil, and jewelry) the day before the wedding and gaze into a full-length mirror. What is the repercussion? The wedding will not come to fruition.

More advice: never get married in velvet, as poverty will follow, and do not include a bird or vine pattern in the dress—it's a recipe for disaster and the marriage will be a long and unhappy one.

Bulletin! Happy wedding-dress beliefs do exist! For luck, a seamstress should sew a piece of the fiancé's hair into the bride's gown. This guarantees a loyal marriage. Furthermore, it is a happy omen to find a spider on the wedding dress on the day of the nuptials. As for fabric and colors, silk is a lucky wedding-gown fabric, and its color should be either white, cream, or ivory. This ensures good luck and a very happy married life. Old wives' tales do foretell that color determines the outlook of the marriage. It is not a wise choice to select black, yellow, green, gray, or pink.

Years ago, when I was shopping for my wedding dress, pale-pink dresses were popular. After shopping for a short time, I found and fell in love with "the dress." The bridal shop had the sample in pink, and after I tried it on, that was the dress I wished to order. Although I adored the pink version, my mother turned that dream into dust by adamantly declaring it was bad luck, and I should order it in white. Yes, I ordered this gown in white. Mother spoke. That was that. I do admit it was lovely in white, yet so unique in pale pink.

The Wedding Ring
Forthcoming nuptials means shopping for the wedding rings. Hooray! (I adore jewelry.) Some couples choose to purchase matching bands, while others do not, and a few opt for sentimental family heirlooms. Even in the event that the wedding-band budget is small, wedding rings are very special, and the selection process is an exciting one.

How did the wedding ring tradition begin? Although it is difficult to pinpoint it precisely, the ancient Egyptians have been given credit. The men uniquely fashioned materials and braided them together to create a special ring for their loves. This act created a sensation that progressed into other civilizations, as the circle represented perpetuity and a long life together, and the hole symbolized eternal love. The early Romans invented the engraving of rings, and later, Christians popularized the wedding band exchange during the marriage ceremony. Over the centuries, the material of the wedding band has evolved, presenting improvements in quality and comfort. Today, the traditional metal used to fashion a wedding ring is platinum, gold, or silver.

Centuries ago, it was deemed lucky to wear the wedding ring on the fourth finger of the left hand, as people thought the vein in that particular finger led directly to the heart. Romans referred to it as the "vein of love." The tradition has endured and is still prevalent today. This is the traditional finger for the wedding ring in the United States and most other cultures.

Conversely, in countries such as Russia, Bulgaria, and Ukraine, bands are placed on the right hand. A friend shared that in the Jewish tradition, the groom will occasionally choose to place the wedding ring on the bride's index finger to ensure good luck.

More lucky ring traditions: the couple places the wedding bands on one another and then they feed one another a sugar cube (to sweeten the marriage). Setting a sapphire in the wedding bands or wearing snake-shaped wedding bands guarantees an eternity of marital bliss.

Over on the unlucky spectrum, pearls added to a wedding band are very unlucky, and if the groom drops the bride's ring during the ceremony, death may result to either party.

Personally, I support the wedding ring tradition. Even so, I feel there is validity to Sam Smith's quote: "I don't understand why you have to wear a wedding ring to warn people off. You should be able to be faithful to that person without anything on your body to show that you are with someone."

My husband wears his wedding ring every day without fail, and is not happy when I forget to wear mine.

The Engagement Ring

Traditionally, an engagement ring is worn prior to the wedding and signifies the wearer is committed. This ring epitomizes a verbal promise. This is a meaningful gift from the groom-to-be to the bride-to-be and is worn on the left hand in Western countries. A friend of mine asked her fiancé to wear a "management ring," which is an engagement ring worn by the man. He declined, saying he did not care to be "managed." Another option is for the couple to wear matching bands during the engagement period.

Typically, the traditional engagement ring has a central diamond or another precious stone and is designed to fit nicely next to the wedding ring. Some brides opt for a wedding set, which is an engagement ring and wedding band fashioned to perfectly fit together. Others, like me, may select a cocktail-style ring, although such a ring doesn't allow room to place the wedding band directly next to it. Brides might wear the engagement ring on the right hand and the wedding band on the left. I choose to wear my wedding band on alternate days.

How Did the Ring Tradition Begin?

The ancient Egyptians and ancient Roman civilizations are given credit for many customs. In this case, the Romans employed a ritual in which the wives wore a ring, which was hooked to a key. (Perhaps a key to one's heart?) This sent a message from the husband to other men that his partner was unavailable.

In the fifteenth century, Archduke Maximilian of Austria introduced the idea of the diamond engagement ring when he commissioned one for his betrothed. The idea seemingly took off, and here we are today with a huge diamond-engagement–ring industry. How much does the average person spend today on a diamond engagement ring? Megan Leonhardt (2018) reported, "The average millennial couple (aged 18–34) spends just over $3,000 on an engagement ring, while the average couple spends about $2,800, according to a TD Bank survey of over 1,700 U.S. adults."

That seems like a conservative number to a New Jersian. However, one does not need to pay a fortune for an engagement ring or feel peer pressure because a neighbor, friend, or relative has been given a very expensive one. If you are currently in the market, I suggest you have fun, take your time, shop around, stop by the diamond districts, invest in a jeweler's loupe, and perhaps buy the setting and stone separately. This may prove to pay off, add to the anticipation, and provide the look you're seeking.

Good Luck and Bad Luck Superstitions Surrounding the Engagement Ring

- Diamonds represent true affection.
- The aquamarine stone represents much luck and happiness, harmony, and a long marriage.
- The emerald ensures a heavenly marriage.
- An old wives' tales says to be careful regarding which day of the week to buy the engagement ring. Saturday is the best choice, as a happy life together is promised. If a ring is purchased on a Monday, look forward to a chaotic marriage.
- An engagement ring in its original setting that has been passed down from one family member to another or one bought in an antique shop carries the luck of the preceding marriage with it. Therefore, if sorrow was attached to it, this will follow the new bride. Conversely, a happy experience formerly will guarantee bliss on the horizon for the newly married couple.
- Pearls bring tears.
- Opals are plain unlucky.
- Never ever let another woman try on your engagement ring. Not only will her vibes attach to the ring, but up the road, she will try to steal the husband.
- It is a bad omen if an engagement ring has a loose stone. (This one must be true, as it would be a costly endeavor to have the stone replaced.)

Which diamond cut is the most popular? According to a jeweler friend, the round cut wins. Next in line is the princess cut, followed by the emerald cut, and then the oval cut. He mentioned a recent trend has been the cushion cut. Personally, I have always adored a heart-shaped stone. Since that cut was low on his sales list, I suppose I'm in the minority.

Celebrity Engagement Rings

An engagement ring is a thrilling piece. This is the ring we show off to our friends immediately following the engagement. It is also a sentimental gift, in some cases passing from one family member to the next. Such was the case with the late Diana, Princess of Wales. Diana's engagement ring was fashioned in eighteen-karat white gold, with an oval blue sapphire as the central stone and fourteen individual diamonds surrounding it. As the story goes, this ring reminded Diana of her own mother's ring. Yet the royal family was perturbed, as it was featured in a catalog, meaning any commoner could purchase one. Loving jewelry and Diana as I do, I purchased my own collector's edition copy.

Later, her firstborn son, Prince William, presented this ring to his fiancée, Kate Middleton, now his famous wife, the Duchess of Cambridge. I've always heard that is unlucky to see the engagement ring before the proposal. In this case, it was not true. Kate has been very fortunate. Moreover, a sapphire engagement ring is supposed to guarantee a happy marriage, so fortunately, none of the ill fortune Diana endured in her marriage will carry over to Will and Kate's. (I loved Princess Diana and enjoyed watching the royal wedding on July 29, 1981.)

In 2017, Princess Diana's son, Prince Harry, proposed to Meghan Markle, and they were wed in 2018. That was an exciting time for all who enjoyed following the wedding. Prince Harry designed the engagement ring himself and included a few of his mother's diamonds. Meghan's ring is set in yellow gold with one large center stone and a smaller diamond on each side that were taken from Diana's personal collection. According to an article in *Money*, "Here's How Much Meghan Markle's Engagement Ring Is Worth" (2017), the jewelry industry claims her ring is "priceless." In this article, Kathryn Money of the jewelry company Brilliant Earth, estimated the ring to be 6.5 carats in total, with the bulk of the carats being the center diamond. Also, Amanda Winters from Blue Nile, an online diamond retailer, claimed, "If the ring included perfect diamonds, it could cost between $300,000 to $350,000. If using mid-range diamonds, it would cost closer to $35,000 to $40,000."

Since Meghan's ring includes Diana's diamonds, it is viewed as invaluable. I'm sure Harry and Megan consider the ring to be very lucky, as the center stone originated from a holiday spot in Botswana, and the others were part of Diana's personal collection. (Yes, I ordered my faux copy of Meghan's ring as well!)

The Elizabeth Taylor Ring
Originally known as the Krupp diamond, it later was coined the "Elizabeth Taylor diamond." In 1968, Richard Burton purchased the diamond for her from an auction. At the time, he paid $307,000 for the 33.19-carat diamond. Later, Liz made it into a signature piece, and it was the favorite in her collection. After her death in 2011, the ring, as well as other items, sold in an auction to a South Korean Corporation. (No, I do not have a copy of the Liz ring.)

Elvis Presley proposed to Priscilla Beaulieu in December 1966. He presented her with a ring with a total of three and half carats in diamonds. The large center diamond was surrounded by a detachable row of smaller diamonds. Elvis loved jewelry and took great pride in his jewelry selections. I would love to have a faux copy of this ring.

Wedding Day Rain
It rained on my wedding day. It was intermittent, though, and we seemed to dodge it. What does wedding day rain indicate? Actually, rain is a good omen, as it is seen as cleansing. If you're extra lucky, a rainbow will peek through the clouds. In the event, you don't want to chance a rainy day, there is a superstitious measure you may try. I have recently learned from a neighbor that placing a statue of the Virgin Mary in the front window of the house during the week preceding the wedding and reciting a daily prayer to Mary guarantees good weather on the wedding day.

As an added measure, a prayer to Saint Claire, the patron saint of good weather in the Philippine tradition, may also help. A Southern tradition suggests burying a bottle of bourbon exactly a month prior to the wedding. (I suggest burying the cheap stuff, not a costly bottle of my husband's favorite, Booker's bourbon.)

The Groom Is Not Allowed to See the Bride before the Wedding
This belief doesn't hold up much in today's society, yet it is one of those superstitions some wish to follow without question, erring on the side of

caution. In the past, this was a strictly followed custom. Often, parents arranged marriages for their sons and daughters with other respected families. Since the couples did not officially meet until the ceremony, it was regarded as unlucky for the prospective groom to see the bride-to-be before the ceremony. It has been said that the father of the bride was afraid that if the prospective groom saw the man's daughter in advance, he might cancel the wedding. This would cause shame to the family. Thank goodness we live in a different age now.

The Bride's Veil
I didn't wear a veil; I felt it would hinder my sight and breathing. Mostly, I wasn't interested in wearing one, although I have known many brides who looked beautiful walking up the aisle with a veil.

Wearing a veil stems from the ancient Romans and Greeks, who thought the veil's material offered protection and shielded the bride from evil unseen forces, jealousy, and overall negative vibes from others. Too bad the veil doesn't guard against mean in-laws.

Tossing the Bridal Bouquet
The bouquet is a featured item in the wedding. The bride, who is the rock star of the day, carries the bouquet. Typically, toward the end of the wedding reception, the bride tosses her bouquet over her head into a crowd of single women who are all vying to catch the flowers. It is alleged that the lucky one who succeeds, will be the next to be married.

I didn't want to part with my bridal bouquet, so my florist created a tinier version to throw into the eager group of women. The practice of tossing the bridal bouquet originated in the medieval period. At that time, this was organized in a different fashion; the guests grabbed at the wedding dress. Those who succeeded were considered lucky to have a piece of the garment. Over time, this evolved into the bride throwing her bouquet, symbolizing tossing good fortune into the crowd while she escaped.

Currently, it is considered an entertaining part of the reception. I have attended a few wedding receptions, however, in which overeager participants knocked others out of the way or cascaded onto the floor in the hope of being the one to catch it.

Carrying the Bride over the Threshold

This is a nice tradition. Upon arriving at home, the gallant groom scoops up the bride and carries her over the threshold of the front doorway. This superstition is taken seriously, even if the couple already resides together. The rationale is that the chivalrous male protects his love by lifting her through the entrance, where evil spirits may be hiding to cause harm to the new bride. Otherwise, she might trip or hurt herself. Yet in Victorian times, the reason for carrying the bride over the threshold was to prove she wasn't too eager to be alone with her husband.

The Wedding Cake

The ancient Romans had a version of the wedding cake. In that era, during the wedding, the family broke a loaf of wheat bread in two over the bride's head. This was a lucky omen and ensured fertility. In later centuries, bread morphed into a wedding pie, referred to as a "bride's pie," and finally evolved into the familiar tiered wedding cake. Old-timers state that the idea for the tiered wedding cake originated from a kissing game the newlyweds would play. The bride and groom would kiss over the top of the cake, then stack the cake higher and higher to see how far they could kiss before it fell to the ground. Sounds messy but fun.

For centuries, the cake has been a staple item of the wedding reception, placed on display and later served to the guests. It signifies the embodiment of a good and sweet life filled with much happiness. Those who enjoy a slice of the cake will receive extra blessings.

When I was little, my mother told me that if I took a piece of the wedding cake home and placed it under my pillow, I would dream of my future husband.

Why do couples save the top tier of the wedding cake for their first anniversary? The tradition is for the bride and groom to eat a piece of the saved cake for their one-year anniversary. This tradition is meant to solidify the marriage and provide luck for many tearless years to come.

A year later, although our cake had been frozen, it tasted disgusting—the price we pay to ensure good luck.

Something Old, Something New, Something Borrowed, Something Blue
You probably have heard the expression, above. What does this represent?

Something old—a mature woman, who has been happily married for a number of years, should lend a fairly old article to the new bride. It epitomizes the same happiness and success the older woman has enjoyed in her marriage and acts as a good luck charm to the new marriage. My mother lent me the small lace handkerchief she carried in her wedding to my father over forty years earlier.

Something new—any new item will suffice—the wedding dress, shoes, or veil. This new item signifies a bright future to the new couple.

Something borrowed—anyone may lend something to the bride; this signifies happiness.

Something blue—this represents wishes for a long-lasting relationship.

My mother was adamant that I carry all four pieces on my wedding day. It's possible, however, for the bride to combine them and carry fewer than four items. For instance, one item may be both borrowed and blue.

Silver sixpence in her shoe—in addition to the bride's wearing or carrying the old, new, borrowed, and blue pieces, it is also lucky to have a silver sixpence in her shoe. The sixpence is a British coin, but a dime or other silver currency may be substituted. It may be sewn into the hem of the dress or tucked into the shoe.

My mother lent me the silver dime she used from her wedding in 1949. I barely noticed it in my fancy rhinestone-laden pump. The coin indicates a prosperous life together. Today, even a lucky penny may be substituted for the silver coin or sixpence, as metal is considered such a vital component to wedding luck.

That is also the reason for the tradition of placing tin cans on the back of the wedding car. Metal is viewed as a vital protector against evil and promotes happiness for the couple.

Kissing Balls, Mistletoe

Kissing balls often are associated with weddings. A kissing ball is a man-made ball fashioned from a choice of different materials (flowers, Styrofoam, etc.) and decorated with ribbons, jewels, or other adornments. Flower girls sometimes carry these down the aisle at the beginning of the wedding. Mistletoe, a popular holiday item that's customarily hung in a doorway, is full of superstition itself. The kissing ball and holiday mistletoe are connected because of mistletoe's magical essence and because more and more weddings incorporate mistletoe in the theme.

Folklore says the Scandinavians created the custom with regard to love and mistletoe after a man came back to life when his love saved him by applying mistletoe berries to his chest. Mistletoe is actually a parasite that grows on oak trees and is poisonous. Some say that the cross used to crucify Jesus was laced with mistletoe, and after the crucifixion, it became toxic. However, it is believed to be lucky in many cultures.

What is the mistletoe superstition? Legend claims when mistletoe is hung in an archway or doorway, any person who passes under it is obliged to give a kiss to the person closest to him or her. I was taught that the one who is standing under the mistletoe is to be kissed. If a person stands beneath the mistletoe and isn't kissed, he or she will never marry. Hanging mistletoe became a popular practice in the nineteenth century, especially during the holiday season.

If you are hoping for a quick kiss from someone special and don't have mistletoe on hand, peel a potato, wrap a string or ribbon around it, and hang it in the doorway. You may wrap sprigs of evergreen or holly around it as well. Allegedly, it has the same power.

Today, the magic remains. The kissing ball is interchangeable with mistletoe as faux mistletoe, and it's also used to represent the kissing tradition.

Random Wedding Superstitions

- If the groom is to remain faithful to his bride, he must have a straight tie during the ceremony. (Can you imagine being the bride and walking up the aisle to a crooked tie?)

- The week of the wedding, the bride should place cat chow in one of her shoes and let a kitty eat the food. This brings good luck. (No thanks.)
- It is lucky to throw rice at the happy couple as they leave the church after the ceremony. This is not a common practice any longer, as there are safer materials to use. There were instances of people slipping on the rice, or the rice inadvertently landing in someone's ear or eye. Rice actually has attracted rodents to the post-wedding scene. More recently, well-wishers throw rose petals or blow bubbles.
- Roses bring good luck and symbolize love.
- Don't get married on the thirteenth. There's no need to say anything more on that score.
- Throwing shoes is an old custom. Groomsmen threw shoes at the newly married couple for good luck. (I wouldn't appreciate that well wish.)
- Whoever makes the first purchase in the marriage will have the voice in the marriage. (This one is appealing for a shopper like me.)
- It is bad luck to receive a knife set as a wedding gift. If so, the relationship will end. I can attest to this, as it happened to a relative.
- English friends have mentioned that Wednesday is a lucky day to get married; marrying on a Monday attracts money, and Saturday is unlucky. Conversely, we Americans love Saturday weddings.
- The reason the bride stands on the left in a Christian ceremony is because in the past, the groom needed space on his right side to fend off other men. That sounds ridiculous, but I would enjoy it.
- Bachelor parties were first held by ancient soldiers, who had a rocking party before getting hitched.

Marriage Rhymes:
My grandmother would recite the following wedding rhymes to me, which she had been taught as a child. As with everything my grandmother told to me, I listened intently.

- Marry in the month of May, and you'll surely rue the day.
- To change the name and not the letter is to change for the worst and not the better.
- Married in yellow, ashamed of your fellow.

- Married in green, ashamed to be seen.
- Married in pink, your spirit will sink.
- Married in gray, you will go far away.
- Married in black, you will wish yourself back.
- Marry in red, and you'll wish you were dead. (Yet in Eastern cultures, red is a lucky wedding dress color.)

Last year I attended a wedding. The groom, who had been previously married a few times, requested that the George Strait song "All My Exes Live in Texas" be played at the reception. The lyrics include the following:

All my exes live in Texas,
And Texas is a place I'd dearly love to be.
But all my exes live in Texas
And that's why I hang my hat in Tennessee.

Personally, I failed to see the humor in that; neither did the bride.

Weddings are an exciting part of life, superstition or not. We may embrace these superstitions, or leave them at the door. After all, becoming engaged should be a joyful and stress-free event. Ultimately, marriage is what you make it. A little lucky charm is always helpful, but don't believe your marriage will fail if these beliefs are not followed. I would not want to find a spider nestled in my wedding dress, no matter how lucky it is. Remember to see them as lighthearted fun or for entertainment, and don't let them rule or ruin your big day.

In Hollywood, brides keep the bouquets and throw away the groom.

—Groucho Marx

Chapter 5

THE EVIL EYE

No one can lie. No one can hide anything, when
he looks directly into someone's eyes.

—Paulo Coelho

In many cultures, the superstition of the evil eye is regarded as one of the very worst. The Italian and Greek societies are two of the more recognized that accept this superstition as truth, but it is taken seriously in many other cultures as well—so much so that the fashion world has made the evil eye a trendy and popular protection item. You can find the evil eye as a tattoo, bracelets, earrings, keychains, and décor.

The Evil Eye
The evil eye is a malicious look or glare that one individual gives to another that sends negativity and harm to that person. Usually, it is rooted in angry thoughts, envy, or jealousy, or a combination of all of these. Some describe it as negative energy, stemming from envy or jealousy, sent through one's eyes and thoughts to another person. Basically, a person's good fortune is at risk after the evil eye has been cast upon him or her, and symptoms appear a short time later. As a result, the stricken individual may feel physically or mentally drained or have a serious headache; overall, things just do not go well in one's life. The recipient has no idea when someone has given him or her the evil eye, as it has no immediate sensation. The evil eye is most likely sent intentionally, although some folks just have the ability to cause

destruction unknowingly by sending this harmful glare. Although termed the evil eye, it is not so much the eye itself but the mind and its thoughts that command the eye.

Difference between Envy and Jealousy
Merriam-Webster defines jealousy as "jealous disposition, attitude, or feeling." (*Merriam-Webster* defines being jealous as "hostile toward a rival or one believed to enjoy an advantage"). It defines envy as "painful or resentful awareness of an advantage enjoyed by another joined with a desire to possess the same advantage, to feel unhappiness over the good fortune of (someone) and desire the same good fortune."

Although envy and jealousy are related, there are differences between the two. Envy means a person wants something tangible that another has in his or her possession. A person may be envious of another's new sports car. On the other hand, jealousy is a fear-based emotion. A person may experience jealousy when he or she fears that someone may take a beloved object or person from his or her life, such as a rival taking away the love of a spouse, partner, friend, or love interest. Other examples: fear of a best friend entering into a new relationship, and the new person becoming a better friend; suspecting a recently hired person at the company may want your job; or fear that an individual wants your love interest.

Both envy and jealousy are negative emotions, but envy is not considered as harmful as jealousy. As a child, I was taught that envy is wishing you had someone's possession but not wishing that person any harm. On the other hand, jealousy is wishing harm to the other person. The evil eye takes into account both envy and jealousy.

The Evil Eye Stare
Old wives' tales indicate that a person might be born with the ability to cast the evil eye, similar to an individual inheriting a psychic skill. Individuals might not realize they have the ability. Some may become aware of it after a few encounters, or a family member might inform them that they can cast the evil eye. Therefore, they might tread lightly, not wishing to cause further ill will to anyone else.

I am told some people are fully aware of their ability to give the evil eye and use it to their advantage. My husband teases me that I have the ability to cast the evil eye on him. He stands by this notion, as he has suffered nose bleeds a few times after we have disagreed. Nosebleeds are uncommon for him, so perhaps I have the ability where he is concerned. (No, I'm teasing.)

Guarding against the Evil Eye

Various societies believe in the legend of the evil eye; thus, various talismans or amulets have been constructed in an effort to shield against the curse it brings. These mostly resemble an eye, but each culture has its differences.

Prayer is a wonderful technique used to shield oneself, as well as to make the effects of the evil eye dissipate. People in the know recite the following three prayers, one after the other: the Lord's Prayer, the Hail Mary, and the Glory Be. Holy water or oil may be used in conjunction with the prayers or alone. The results of the evil eye eventually will go away, but dissipates much quicker by praying.

Sadly, it is possible that an animal may be given the evil eye by a person who has become annoyed or doesn't like the pet. This is difficult to imagine and upsetting to me that a defenseless animal could be a recipient. My Irish grandmother explained the process of curing a household pet that received the evil eye. If you suspect the evil eye has been cast on your precious friend, immediately apply the following Irish remedy:

- The animal's owner must draw a cross on a blank piece of white paper three times. This can be done in an up, down, or across fashion.
- Recite a prayer.
- Scatter holy water across the paper.
- Burn the paper, and strew the smoke gently around the pet.

Recipient of the Evil Eye

If you suspect you have received the evil eye but are not quite sure, try this simple test: place three drops of olive oil into a small bowl. If the oil forms into an eye shape, you are the recipient of the evil eye. Counteract it by praying the three prayers, as mentioned earlier. If no eye appears, thank your lucky stars that this feeling was only a false alarm.

Irish, Italian, Greek, and Jewish Evil Eye Beliefs

Cultural differences exist with regard to the evil eye, yet it all boils down to the same philosophy. It is caused by envy and jealousy, and ill-fated symptoms arise. The differences in the evil eye beliefs in Greece, Italy, and Ireland and in Judaism are discussed below.

Greece

The Greek term for the evil eye is *mati*, and it's an ancient and serious belief in this culture. Greeks subscribe to a ritual of warding off the evil in order to live a normal life. In Greece, the protection worn is a blue-eyed charm or a blue bead fashioned into a charm as a piece of jewelry or decor. Some Greeks believe that special spiritual personalities have the ability to recite formal prayers and release the ill effects caused by the evil eye. Staunch believers even integrate an evil eye tradition into the wedding celebration. During the nuptials, the bride will touch a blue article placed on her dress to counteract any jealousy from anyone in the crowd.

Also, Greeks suggest that new mothers remain inside their residences for at least a month with the newborn. They think that some baby well-wishers are filled with negative thoughts and will send harm to the little one, which is especially dangerous for an infant in his or her vulnerable stage of life. Furthermore, if someone gives a compliment to the baby, and it is not followed by the phrase "God bless you," this spells danger. Immediately, the parent must utter a spitting sound to counteract the evil that has been cast on the child.

Italy

In Italy, the word *malocchio* refers to the evil eye. In America, Italians refer to it as the *maloik*. Indications of being a recipient of the maloik are a severe headache, unnecessary constant yawning, and a feeling of lethargy. The recipient may experience one or all of these warning signs. The feeling may be stronger and last longer if the recipient is a sensitive person or if the evil eye is sent with extreme intention.

Years ago, I attended the wedding shower of a friend, Giovanni, which was held at her parents' house. She and her family are 100 percent Italian and speak the language fluently. The majority of the group were Italian women, except for a few of us. The food was spectacular, her parents were friendly, and the opening of the gifts was very enjoyable. The person I came with, Shirley, and I had a fantastic time—or so we thought.

Afterward, as Shirley and I were riding home together, I remarked that I had a terrible headache and my eyes were very blurry, so I was glad she was driving. Shirley was yawning almost the entire drive and seeming sluggish. We thought nothing of it, attributing our conditions to the wine we'd had or to our overeating. Later that week, when I saw Giovanni, I joked that Shirley and I had been such big party-goers that we'd felt sick on the way home. She studied my face intently and asked about our symptoms. When I explained, Giovanni said that someone had given the evil eye to us at the party. This was my first real experience with the evil eye, and I remember thinking it was powerful.

Luckily, Giovanni said it would burn off after a while, and it already had by the time I spoke to her. Still, the damage already done was no fun. Later, she bought me an evil eye amulet for protection. "It's effective only when it is gifted," she told me, "and ineffective when a person buys it for himself or herself."

In the Italian culture, people ward off the evil eye by wearing a small horn, termed a *cornicello*. Italian-Americans also wear evil eye jewelry to remain protected against evil forces.

Ireland

The Irish refer to the evil eye as *drochshúil*. This is a combination of the words evil and eye. The act of causing harm to someone with just a wee glance goes back centuries in Ireland. The evil eye is very well known in Irish folklore and also is documented in Irish writings, including an essay by folklorist Alexander Haggerty Krappe:

The Irish evil eye amulet resembles an open eye in the middle of a round piece of metal or jewelry. Celtic knots, crosses and shamrocks are used for protection to guard against people and their wicked wrath.

I know the methods the Irish employ to counteract the evil eye, as my Irish grandmother resided in Ireland as a youngster. After she moved to the United States, she offered authentic remedies for pets and to others who needed counsel. Of course, I jotted these into my journal, although I was not too interested; I couldn't ever remember having an incident until Giovanni's shower. Since that time, however, I consider it critical information.

Earlier, I referenced a method my grandmother used to lift the evil eye from an animal. Since my grandmother was surrounded by farmlands and animals in Ireland, she was schooled in the technique. She mentioned that she was in the habit of reciting prayers to shield animals in the pasture from any evil eye. Her mother had explained that individuals often sent the evil eye to these unsuspecting creatures because they were jealous of the farmer's livestock.

The following was her Irish protection prayer: "May God's blessing be placed on and protect all living creatures who are helping feed the people."

She also told me of a prayer that is instrumental in shielding beloved household pets: "God bless his creatures who bring so much joy to this earth."

For humans, if you suspect you know who cast the evil eye, repeating the initial of his or her first name will nullify it. Repeat every initial if you feel it helps!

Judaism
In the Hebrew language, the word that translates to the evil eye is *ayin ha'ra*. It is the power of directing a mere gaze to another, causing negativity and harm. The evil eye is a superstition in the Jewish culture and is revealed in rabbinic texts.

What are the Jewish beliefs for protecting oneself? The following are ways to skirt the evil eye:

The Jewish tradition uses a talisman, a *hasma,* to shield against disaster. This amulet resembles a hand with five fingers extended, with an eye placed in its palm.

In ancient times, if someone feared he or she had received the glare, the person would immediately spit on the ground three times to negate it.

A friend explained that his parents use the following sentence when discussing any upcoming plans: "Let it be without the evil eye." This ensures that anyone who has knowledge of their plans and casts the evil eye, due to envy or jealousy, will not ruin them. For instance, if a couple who are planning to build a new house recite this evil-averting phrase, it will be safe against delays, mishaps, and the like. I love that phrase and try to employ it as often as I can.

It's ironic how one person's gaze can send much so love and tenderness to us or, conversely, such evil wishes. If we all operate with grateful hearts, however, and send out our very best vibes and intentions to others each day, we will receive that in return, and life will not contain the evil eye. Good luck to all of us.

The face is a mirror of the mind, and eyes without
speaking confess. The secrets of the heart.

—Saint Jerome

Chapter 6

BIRDS AND SUPERSTITION

Birds are indicators of the environment.
If they are in trouble, we know we'll soon be in trouble.

—Roger Tory Peterson

Birds are mostly regarded as serene creatures. It can be a beautiful sight to gaze upon them as they play happily in a bird bath. It's fascinating to watch them as they migrate south for the winter, and it's peaceful to listen to their charming melodies. On the other hand, birds sometimes are considered shadowy and ominous, and they offer great mystery to the world.

Birds have always had an important role on this planet. For centuries, civilizations consulted birds for answers to questions regarding life, love, health, death, wealth, and luck, to name a few topics. Legend depicts birds as ethereal creatures that are allowed to pass between here and the netherworld. People once thought that birds were sent by gods, or they thought that birds were gods themselves, as they had the power to fly and soar high into the sky. This belief likely developed from the simple fact that birds can fly. Several gods have been depicted as birds, such as the Egyptian gods Horace and Isis. The Norse god Odin is also depicted as a bird.

Our ancestors claim all birds impart predictions to us, and we should pay attention to their messages. The Native American and Celtic cultures allege that birds delivered messages to humans through patterns of flight. It's amazing that the behavior that our forefathers observed has been carried into today's scientific world through these theories, secret codes, and messages.

In this chapter, we will explore eight types of birds: the raven, hawk, crow, albatross, peacock, owl, and hummingbird and the mammal bat. Each offers its own superstitious beliefs, omens, communication, and special meanings.

Raven

The mystique of the raven is very powerful and considered lucky by English royalty. In former centuries, ravens were known to be the birds known to live in towers, thereby coined the "Guardians of the Tower." Royals felt that if these birds were to leave, the Tower of London would fall victim to bad luck. In the 1600s, King Charles II was deathly afraid that if the ravens who lived at the Tower ever left, his empire would crumble immediately. For hundreds of years, the ravens have been encouraged to stay, and today, there are seven in residence at the Tower. These feathered friends have an especially pampered life.

For those of us outside the United Kingdom, ravens offer other benefits. They are visionary creatures; therefore, dreaming of one holds a special meaning—that change is approaching, for example, or that someone is taking advantage of you. The Romans took heed in the powers of the raven and studied their flight patterns for answers to their dilemmas. Romans assumed if a blind person was kind to a raven, that individual might regain his or her sight.

Crow

For the most part, the crow is the foreteller of death. Superstitious types cower when encountering this bird. It's especially unlucky if you spot a crow on your property, as it can mean the potential death of someone in the home. How can you protect your household? Immediately salute or bow to the crow; it may take mercy on you and your loved ones.

Moreover, never kill a crow, since it may result in your untimely demise. If you do kill a crow, wear black, bury it respectfully, and hope the other crows will forgive you. On a happy note, if you see a crow, whisper a secret wish to it, and it may be granted.

Farmers thought that witnessing a crow flying from the east to the west meant a healthy crop. That seems lucky!

Ravens and crows are commonly thought be the same bird. They are part of the same scientific classification family, but there are differences. Ravens are bigger than crows and prefer private dwellings.

Hawk
The hawk is a large and powerful bird with keen eyesight. Hawks symbolize wisdom and spiritual vision. Spotting a hawk is a sign from the divine. It suggests a new duty is coming into your life, such as a leadership role. The hawk is promising that you are ready to soar! The hawk is a bird of prey. Old wives' tales warn never to leave small dogs or babies unattended, as the hawk has the power to carry away a being of that weight.

Albatross
The albatross has an extensive wing span. It is a beautiful sight to see one in flight. In years past, sailors used the albatross as a barometer. If albatross surrounded the ship, bad weather was approaching. Mariners took a dim view of the killing of any bird and especially an albatross, since that was viewed as highly unlucky; furthermore, the ship could be lost at sea. Now, with modern instruments, sailors no longer rely on the albatross.

The term to "an albatross around your neck" means to carry a heavy burden. Those who intentionally or unintentionally slay an albatross will carry some type of burden throughout life. This expression is still popular today.

Peacock
The peacock is native to sections of western China and is known for its elegance and splendor. The peacock (the male of the species) displays its beautiful tail feathers to attract the female birds (peahens). Most people feel peacock feathers carry good fortune. Some say these feathers may cure

a broken heart if you place one near your heart. Feathers may be used to enhance an outfit or hat or as home décor, as their brilliance attracts good luck. Peacocks were considered sacred in Greek and Roman mythology due to their great knowledge and a divine sense of seeing (the peacock eyes in the feather). Because the evil eye may be seen in the feathers, the feathers ward off evil spirits.

In Hindu lore, the peacock is linked with the goddesses who demonstrated compassion and humanity toward others.

Buddhists believe that since peacocks may eat poisonous plants and survive, they embody immortality.

However, there exists a negative school of thought concerning the peacock. Theater people will not wear a costume with peacock feathers for fear of a bad performance. In the past, farmers would not allow a peacock indoors, as it meant their daughters would turn into grouchy spinsters. Peacocks are thought to attract poverty.

One thing is certain: no one can dispute the radiance and wow factor of the peacock.

Owl
The owl holds positive and negative aspects. On a positive note, an owl is a font of wisdom and insight. Old wives' tales suggest that to aid poor vision, consume an owl's eggs, and sipping owl-egg broth can calm a cough and even keep seizures at bay. People generally adore the owl for its beauty and keen senses, and its many spiritual gifts. It brings good luck to keep a white owl statue in the home.

On the negative side, owls foretell death. To hear an owl hooting means the Grim Reaper is near. This stems from the death of Julius Caesar, when an owl purportedly hooted before he died. The owl who screeches is not as ominous as one who hoots but still is considered unlucky. Finally, it is unlucky to see an owl during daylight.

Hummingbird

The hummingbird is revered for its resiliency and swiftness. This stunning bird is often associated with the Native American culture, which believes that hummingbirds bring a harmonious balance to the earth. In folklore, the hummingbird is a bearer of good tidings, and when spotted, it is always a positive message. If a hummingbird lands and lingers nearby, this may indicate that a departed spirit is sending love, that a new love interest is on the way, or that heavenly help is on the way in answer to a worrisome problem. Overall, these creatures symbolize love, good luck, synchronization, and healing.

Bats

Centuries ago, the bat was thought to be a bird that did not have feathers. Even though bats are mammals, I've included the bat in this section. The word *bat* generally conjures a feeling of eeriness, thoughts of vampires, and, on a health note, rabies. Since bats are creatures of the night, and some think they are linked to witches, there is a natural psychological fear of them. Right off the bat (no pun intended), the bat is naturally considered a bad omen. In actuality, however, bats are beneficial to society.

According to "Top 5 Benefits of Bats" by Rob Ripma (2015), bats offer the five advantages listed below:

1. A bat may consume up to 1,200 insects in one hour.
2. Some bats pollinate the seeds and fruits we humans consume.
3. The fruit bat is critical to the dispersal of seeds.
4. Bat droppings may act as fertilizer.
5. Some folks are awed by bats.

In fact, a bat tourist attraction exists in Austin, Texas, and approximately one hundred thousand tourists travel there each year. These travelers gather near a bridge where thousands of bats reside just to watch the bats exit the bridge in the evening.

I grew up on a farm and enjoyed a wonderful childhood full of pets, fresh air, and walks in the woods. The one thing I did not adore, however, was the seemingly hundreds of bats that housed themselves in the barn roof near our house and flew out each day at dusk. I would run into the house quickly as they swooped toward my hair. I was frightened that one would get caught in my hair (another old wives' tale). I also learned to leave the swimming pool at twilight for the same reason. When I was young, I didn't realize the bats were merely trying to catch a mosquito for their breakfast. Still, I am not compelled to take a trip to the tourist attraction in Austin.

Bat omens include the following:

- If a bat enters the home and flies in a circle three times, a death in the family is imminent.
- A bat spotted outside, flying fancifully about, means good weather on the horizon.
- Bats are aligned with witches or turn into vampires; they all represent evil.
- It is bad luck to kill a bat, and to do so means one's life will be shortened.
- To see a bat hanging in the kitchen is good luck.
- If a bat flies toward a light, it is seen as unlucky.
- If a bat circles a woman's head three times, a baby is on the way.
- A bat who flies into the house has been invited in by a ghost who is attached to the residence.

If you see a bat on your premises, do not attempt to kill it. Please trap it, and call an animal control center immediately. They will remove it safely.

Below, I have included an old-fashioned, silly bat rhyme that my grandmother learned as a child in Ireland. Whenever she visited us on the farm, as the bats exited the barn at dusk, she would recite it to me. If we actually had offered bread to the bats, a few loaves would have been required!

> Airy mouse, airy mouse, fly over my head.
> And you shall have a crust of bread.

General Bird Behavior

What does it mean when a bird flies into your house? Is it senseless to think that it automatically spells disaster? Folklore, old wives' tales, and grandmothers say it all depends on the type of bird. For instance, a turtle dove is not one we would wish to enter our homes, as it is the predicator of money woes.

It is also considered unlucky to have a pet bird in the house. I'm not in agreement with this superstition, as each day people offer their homes to beautiful birds who become precious pets. The indoor-bird mind-set extends to bird wallpaper, decor, and/or images.

If you are a Lucille Ball fan, then you may know she had a bird superstition. Lucy was fearful and cautious about birds and having any bird paraphernalia in her home. Moreover, she would never stay in a hotel or visit anyone who displayed bird wallpaper.

I have wondered about the luck attached to the birds that fly freely about shopping malls. If superstition holds true—that birds indoors are unlucky—it's no wonder the malls across America are dying off due to online shopping.

Birds Hitting a Windshield
A bird hitting a vehicle's windshield is placed in the same category as one entering the home—not good! The reality is that as the bird catches a glimpse of its reflection in the glass, it assumes it is another bird. This sorry birdie is only trying to warn the other one (only its reflection) that the territory belongs to him, and he meets his demise as a result.

One day as my husband was having his auto glass repaired (not from a bird but a stone), the repairer and I began discussing birds flying into windshields. This man—someone employed in the auto glass business—mentioned that millions of birds meet their end each year by hitting glass, not necessarily just vehicle glass but windows overall.

Bird Pecking on the Window
Beware! A bird pecking at the window foretells death to someone who occupies the home.

Seeing a Dead Bird
Seeing a dead bird seems to suggest a bad omen, but actually, it is quite the opposite. It suggests a happy change is coming, or a life's struggle is

coming to an end. This is positive news for me, as I have stumbled often upon deceased birds while walking my doggie-daughter, Mimi.

Predicting the Future

The ancient Romans believed birds could predict the future. They observed birds, determined the flight patterns, used the data to answer difficult questions, and choose the best course of action. This technique is called *augury*. Whether the bird flew right or left, fast or slow, it provided answers and wisdom and determined good or bad luck. Birds were not perceived as taboo in Roman society. After all, the birds were linked to gods and were bestowed with knowledge and critical information. The mere fact they could fly gave them power.

Augury

Merriam-Webster's Dictionary gives an example of augury in the following sentence: "Ancient *augury* involved the interpretation of the flight patterns of birds." In addition to the Romans, the Celts applied this to answer life's dilemmas.

Today, we may try this process to answer a few burning questions and for fun. To be effective, we must engage our intuition while watching a pattern of birds in flight.

Steps to take when using augury are as follows:

- Take a few moments to relax and carve out a comfortable spot outside. Do not have any distractions nearby, such as your cell phone. Ask your question mentally.
- Gaze up into the clear sky. It is best to do this in a season when birds heavily travel in flocks, but you can do it with only a few birds flying together.
- Unwind, and do not rush. The birds naturally will come into sight.
- Mentally log what you notice about the birds in flight. In which direction are they flying? Are they flying easily, with difficulty or determination, in a straight line, or flying about?

- Use your instinct to give meaning to their actions. Decipher what this group of birds' motions mean to you and your current inquiry or situation.
- The key is to be open-minded and to take in everything the birds are telling you. Watch, listen, and feel.

For example, your question may involve partaking in a risky financial venture. If the birds fly haphazardly, the answer would indicate no. If the flight pattern is smooth and consistent, a yes answer would be the obvious one.

This is an enjoyable exercise, and practice makes perfect. Remember, though, it's for entertainment purposes only.

Random Bird Superstitions

- A bird in the house, desperately searching for an exit, is extending the message to free yourself of a current, unhealthy situation.
- It is lucky to have bird droppings fall on your head.
- If you encounter a magpie, tip your hat, or give it a curtsey in order to avoid bad luck.
- Be kind to a robin; whatever you do or wish upon it will return to you.
- One of the luckiest birds is a kingfisher.
- Beware if you notice three seagulls directly over your head, for a death will occur.
- Do not kill a sparrow, as each one carries a soul of the deceased.
- A severe storm is approaching if a swan places its head and neck over the rest of its body at dusk.
- Sailors should have a wren on board ship, as it will protect those sailing from drowning.
- Native Americans believe in listening to nature and being open to its messages. Birds provide this through their overall actions.
- If a bird follows you, you have a mystical spirit guide.
- Vultures appear scary, but their commanding message is to make the best of every situation.
- To find a bird's feather means a message from an angel or a deceased loved one.

Superstitions are often a way of explaining odd or strange events, and they began during times when science was unable to explain them. Advancements in scientific knowledge, however, explain much more. As we have seen, some superstitions portray certain types of birds as unseemly creatures. Yet each bird has a mission and is truly a wonderful addition to this planet. Birds offer us beauty and song and are a pleasure to have in our sky and on earth. We have been fortunate to have our feathered friends among us in the past, currently, and—I'm positive—way into the future.

If I had to choose, I would rather have birds than airplanes.

—Charles Lindbergh

Chapter 7

SUPERSTITIONS SURROUNDING THE CANINE AND THE FELINE

Women and cats will do as they please, and men and
dogs should relax and get used to the idea.

—Robert A. Heinlein

Believe it or not, some of the strangest superstitions are with regard to our furry friends. In ancient times, many cultures regarded animals, especially the dog and the cat, as very special, highly revered, and powerful beings. As you will soon learn, these trusted pets, with their heightened senses and watchful natures, even influenced human behavior, including actions regarding superstition.

Canines
How many dogs exist in the United States and the world as a whole?
I believe it is safe to say that canine superstitions will continue as long as dogs exist in this world, regardless of statistics. Yet it's interesting to note the number of dogs among us. In 2018, Martin Fix reported the overall statistics in the article, "How Many Dogs Are There in the World?"

It's estimated that there are 900 million dogs in the world, as of 2018. Of these approximately 3/4 of these are free-range dogs (which also includes feral and wild dogs).

According to Statista.com, "In 2017, a total of about 89.7 million dogs lived in households in the United States as pets. In comparison, some 68 million dogs were owned in the United States in 2000."

In my opinion, dogs make fabulous pets and certainly become members of the family. Their presence is invaluable. Dogs are ready to protect us, physically and emotionally, by offering us peace or helping us through troubling times. It is heartbreaking to watch commercials depicting homeless and abused dogs. I find it worthwhile to contribute a percentage of my paycheck to help these helpless animals. Recently, my husband and I rescued a cute little doggie. We named her Little Bacca because she resembles Chewbacca from the movie *Star Wars*.

Howling Doggies
Legend states when a dog is howling, it is an unlucky omen. There is no question that when a dog is howling very late at night, especially in the distance, it conjures all sorts of unnerving thoughts.

What does a dog's howling foretell?

- Howling for no apparent reason indicates spirits are in the nearby area.
- If howling occurs in the close vicinity of a sick person, it forecasts death.
- A dog's howling four times in succession signals a death has transpired, and the news will arrive shortly. If this howling is specifically done at night, the death of a friend is imminent.
- Spotting a dog in an intersection while it is howling means it is summoning Hecate, the ancient Greek goddess. She is the goddess of the crossroads and is very protective. In some early writings, she was described as having three heads, one being that of a dog.

When I was a teenager, my boyfriend's dog was a beagle named Ringer, and he howled constantly. The first time I heard Ringer howl, I was frightened, thinking he was predicating something awful. Shortly thereafter, I learned that breed of dog is known to regularly howl, so I was relieved. (Of course, there may be exceptions.) However, at the time, I was not aware of this beagle behavior and was consumed with worry that evening. That can kill the mood of any date.

Doggie Talking a Walk
Have you ever witnessed a dog merrily trotting along between two walkers? If so, it foretells an ill-fated couple, whose dating days will never take them to the altar together. If the two are already married, they are safe from divorce. I cringe when I am out walking and witness this scenario if I don't know if the couple is dating or wed. Realistically, most dogs are alpha and tend to lead their masters, so no worries.

Meeting a Stranger Doggie
Legend holds if an individual comes across a stray dog and it follows that person, good luck will also follow. If a strange dog enters the house with you, it is extra lucky. When I was thirteen years old, I befriended a stray puppy I'd met in the woods near my house. She was a wonderful dog, and I loved her so much. I named her Lucky.

Dogs Serving as Weather Reporters
Bad weather on the horizon? Your pooch knows. If he or she ducks under a table or takes shelter elsewhere in the house suddenly, a severe storm is brewing. I notice my small dog, Mimi, will shiver before a rainstorm. Additionally, if the dog crosses its front paws or eats grass, or you wash your doggie, rain is on the way.

Black Dogs
Some folks consider the black dog, as with the black cat, to be unlucky. If a black cat crosses your path, it is not a good sign; the black dog delivers the same forecast. Personally, I find black cats and dogs very attractive.

Seeing the Unknown
Dogs protect us from the unknown. Old-timers say it's a good practice to place a dog by the bed of a sick or dying person. This is because this animal has the ability to see the unknown and will guard the ill person against evil forces that may be hovering. Dogs are very perceptive and have the ability

to see and hear much more than a human. The dog who has seven toes is the most perceptive of all.

In the event your four-legged friend is startled, growls, or stares at something you cannot see, a ghost is most likely present. Years ago, my husband and I lived in a seventeenth-century house, which regularly had ghostly occurrences. One day, our beloved German shepherd, Dutch, was sitting in the kitchen with us. Suddenly, he became startled, turned his head, stared at something we could not see, and backed away from the table quickly. I remember this specifically, and I still think about it to this day. Good thing Dutch was with us, or who knows? Sadly, Dutch has since passed away, and we miss him terribly. He was fifteen years old, which is a long life for a shepherd. A friend who is a psychic medium assures me that Dutch occasionally visits.

Healing Abilities
Canines are used as comfort dogs for the ill in hospitals. Their presence certainly uplifts the patients' spirits and aids the healing process. A friend who has volunteered in a local hospital said that often, after certain patients pet a dog, their blood pressure lowers. In ancient Rome, it was believed that a canine's lick could cure an ailment or wound.

Heavenly Dogs
When it is our time to enter heaven's pearly gates, our deceased dogs will push to the front of the line of those who are waiting for us. That gives me a happy feeling. In earlier days, it was understood that an individual's departed dog(s) would come to the death bed and guide him or her to heaven to ensure a safe journey, with no evil experiences along the way.

Miscellaneous Dog Beliefs

- White and spotted dogs are especially lucky.
- Spotting three white dogs together is a good omen.
- It is lucky to own a greyhound with a single white spot on its head.
- If your dog does not care for a particular person, he or she knows that person's true personality. A friend, Sheila, truly subscribes to this superstition. On any first date, she will introduce a potential boyfriend to her pet bulldog, Gypsy. Gypsy has proven highly

accurate in determining if the person is worth keeping or should be tossed. (Good dog! You deserve a bone or two!)

- If the inside of your dog's mouth is pure black, it offers spiritual protection when you are in its company.
- A sick baby who has been licked by a dog will heal easily.
- An ill infant may be cured by the mystical powers of the dog if the dog is fed some of the baby's hair between slices of white bread.
- If you see a black dog without its owner while you're driving, beware of an auto accident.
- Seamen believe it is unlucky to take a canine on board the vessel.
- The Sumerians believed in a goddess named Bau, who is the protector of all canines. She has been depicted with two heads and is part woman and part dog. Bau supposedly has many dogs buried around the remains of her temple.

Dogs are purely a gift from heaven. They are brave and loyal; they love us unconditionally and offer so many benefits to this world.

Cats
Felines project a great deal of beauty as well as mystery and are steeped in superstition.

A Brief History of the Evolution of Cats
Today's domesticated cat is a subspecies of the wildcat. Since many have interbred over time, it is difficult to pinpoint exactly which cat began it all, yet most have likely originated from the North African and European areas. Large cats survived by hunting birds and other wildlife and were similar to our smaller version today. As the cat evolved over the centuries, it developed a relationship with humans, as the cat willingly lived near the villages and protected the villagers from rats and other dangers. In ancient Egypt, they were quite the protector, killing snakes and harmful bugs that might have ruined the grain and hurt humans. They were rewarded with table scraps, and eventually, humans began adopting them as pets, as the relationship was a win/win. The pet cats were so adored that some were associated with gods and even were depicted in artwork. Sadly, during the Middle Ages and Salem witchcraft era, cats were associated with witchcraft and were hunted. In the 1800s, cats experienced a renaissance

and were once again deeply cared for and treated like members of the family.

Interestingly, after years of families using ashes or sand as kitty litter, the real McCoy was finally professionally developed in the 1940s. I am happy to report cats are here to stay.

How many cats are house pets in the United States?

According to a statistica.com article, "Pets: Number in the U.S. by Species 2017/2018" (2018), "In 2017 the total number of cats owned as a pet in the United States amounted to about 95.6 million." Certainly, that is a great number of kitties and does not even count the undomesticated feline.

Nine Lives
Most of us have heard the old wives' tale that a cat has nine lives since cats always land on their feet and has the knack to survive perilous situations that normally would harm other types of animals. Cats have keen senses, are very agile, and are equipped with survival tools such as claws and sharp teeth.

Cats often can survive alone in the outdoors much easier than dogs. I often notice them roaming around happily without an owner, which is not common for dogs, who usually are on leashes.

In the sixteenth century, William Shakespeare mentioned a cat's nine lives in his play *Romeo and Juliet*. One of the characters, Mercutio, speaks the following line: "Good King of Cats, I want to take one of your nine lives."

Today, some folks use this expression more loosely and apply it to other settings that are not related to cats. For instance, a person may feel he or she has nine lives after surviving a perilous situation.

Cats and Babies
Several old wives' tales center on cats and babies together. One is that if the household cat sniffs the baby, the baby will grow up to be fearless. A scary myth is that if a black cat is left alone with a baby, it may suck the breath or life from the infant. This is an unpleasant thought that, in reality,

is highly unlikely. Still, no matter how friendly your house cat, I would suggest erring on the side of caution and placing the cat and the baby at a safe distance from each other. The cat may feel playful and jump at or scratch the infant, or it may feel jealousy toward the new member of the household.

Moving

Those who own a cat and have moved from residence to residence can appreciate that these creatures do not adjust well or quickly to their new digs. Good news—old wives' tales suggest that this behavior may be offset by trying one or both of the following tricks: When relocating, do not bring your cute fur ball into the residence in the traditional way. Rather, gently shove the cat through a window. Since a cat is curious by nature, this tactic will likely ease it into its new environment and help it to overcome any nervousness. The second trick is to coat the feline's paws with an edible treat, such as kitty food or soft butter. This will entertain the cat and keep it preoccupied, although it may stain a new carpet.

Do you agree with this logic? It's worth a try, even though cats are not easily fooled. We do love our pets and will take any measures to ensure their happiness.

Random Cat Beliefs

- Cats have the ability to forecast the weather. Pressing its nose to the window indicates rain is on the way.
- A cat sitting with its back to the fireplace means a chilly day is approaching.
- Cats can predict when a visitor will arrive. If the kitty wipes its face with its paws, a relative will arrive shortly. Whisker cleaning indicates a religious person will soon ring the doorbell.
- To dream of a white kitty cat is good luck, but beware if one is spotted while the sun is setting.
- Cats may attract fortune. Felines with light-colored fur attract money and decrease debt. Cats with dark-colored fur bring wealth.

In the Japanese culture, displaying a Maneki-Neko (a common cat figurine) in the home or business is thought to attract prosperity.

• In ancient Egypt, cats were regarded as spiritual and magical creatures. If one was intentionally hurt, a mysterious illness would befall the person who inflicted the pain. Some people still think this is true. My grandmother told me that in Ireland, it's whispered that those who harm a cat will endure fifteen years of bad luck, and if a man deliberately steps on a cat's tail, he will never find the love of his life.

The mystique of the cat is undeniable.

I am a firm believer that cats and dogs enhance our lives. I enjoyed growing up surrounded by them, and they added much happiness to my life. They are very special creatures, sent to us from above, with a mission to protect, offer comfort, provide emotional support through painful times, and be an overall joy for us. In turn, we spoil them and offer protection. I wish the life spans of dogs and cats were much longer.

Owners of dogs have noticed that, if you provide them with food and water and shelter and affection, they will think you are God. Whereas owners of cats are compelled to realize that, if you provide them with food and water and affection, they draw the conclusion that they are God.

—Christopher Hitchens

Chapter 8

GEMSTONES AND SUPERSTITION

I adore wearing gems but not because they are mine. You
can't possess radiance; you can only admire it.

—Elizabeth Taylor

Superstition and gemstones appear to go hand in hand. For centuries,
numerous cultures have placed faith in gems, either in a positive or negative
sense. Bad luck is connected with many stones. Conversely, other stones
have the green light and aid in the protection against evil forces and attract
good luck; some have been assigned a great deal of spiritual power. Gems
have been placed as adornments on shielding talismans or amulets, crosses,
and religious articles in order to make them blessed focal points.

Let's explore the two schools of thought: the lucky and unlucky gems.

Unlucky Gems
The Opal
The opal has a bad reputation and is, in fact, called the "stone of tears."
The black opal is especially unlucky. Overall, it is not advisable to give
or receive this stone. If you happen to receive an opal, try to gracefully
decline it to avoid the bad tidings to come. If you absolutely must accept
it, give the gift-giver a quarter, and that act will negate the opal's negative
energy—that seems like an easier task than declining the present.

When I was ten years old, my oldest brother gave me an opal necklace. It was so pretty, and I was thrilled, but my mother demanded he exchange it for something else. Only after that time did I learn of the twenty-five-cent method.

The Curse of the Hope Diamond

The Hope diamond is a very large blue gem that is over forty-five carats in weight. It is probably the most well-known cursed gemstone. In the nineteenth century, it acquired its name from Henry Thomas Hope. After Hope passed away, the diamond later was owned by several other people. Legend tells that the diamond owners endured perilous events in their lives, including suicide, murder, and monetary loss, to name only a few. Supposedly, suffering accompanies the diamond. It has been rumored that the Hope diamond was on the *Titanic,* but that is untrue.

Centuries earlier, this stone was part of the statue of a holy idol in India. It was stolen, and the thief, a Hindu priest, met an untimely and horrifically slow death. Since that time, the gem has been considered cursed.

It eventually found its way to Europe, where it was sold to Louis XIV of France in 1668. He died of gangrene. The gem remained part of royal jewelry, and later, this cursed stone came into the possession of King Louis XVI and his wife, Marie Antoinette. Both were eventually beheaded.

The stone disappeared from view for a while and eventually ended up in the hands of Henry Thomas Hope. Even with its cursed reputation, Hope doesn't seem to have encountered any misfortune. Today, the Hope diamond is safely located in the National Museum of Natural History in Washington, DC.

Pearls

Pearls symbolize tears and are best not bestowed as gifts, as they bring sadness to the recipient. It's best not to incorporate pearls into an engagement or wedding ring; as the expression goes, they bring "tears to the marriage." Brides are particularly cautioned against wearing pearls on their wedding day, whether as jewelry or on the dress, veil, or shoes, lest they begin their new lives with sorrow.

Lucky Gems
A more pleasant subject focuses on the gemstones that are not cursed.

The Emerald
Emeralds are full of good luck. Expectant mothers who don an emerald will feel less pain and little morning sickness. Other positives: emeralds keep away witches, and if you need to go to court, wearing one will ensure victory.

The Ruby
It is rumored a ruby will change its color, depending on the health of the person wearing it. The richer the color, the healthier the person; the weaker the shade, the unhealthier the person.

When I was twelve, I loved to wear my mood ring, which reflected the color of my current disposition. The ruby reminds me of a mood ring of sorts. Also, the ruby guards against receiving unkind thoughts projected from another person.

The Sapphire
The sapphire is associated with happiness and true love. If a man woos his love with a sapphire, he will live in her heart forever.

The Topaz
The topaz is my birthstone, and I'm happy to report it is considered good luck. I don't really care for the appearance of the stone, but I should wear one, as it attracts money and power. Plus, if confronted by a wild animal, this stone has the power to calm it.

Jade
Jade is extremely lucky. It symbolizes fertility, peacefulness, and good health. It is a popular stone that artisans often fashion into bracelets, rings, and pendants.

Turquoise
This stone is a mixture of green and blue. It associated with serenity and has a calming effect on its wearer. It also represents good luck and is commonly fashioned into jewelry in the Southwest. In ancient cultures,

it was a symbol of wealth. The spiritual world connects turquoise with psychic protection.

Crystals

Crystals are very positive stones, and many people are fascinated by them. There are many uses for crystals—psychic awareness, physical healing, chakra balancing, feng shui, spiritual development, warding off evil spirits, and cleansing a living space or oneself. Today, crystals are revered, but in earlier times, they had a bad reputation as being evil and were used solely for sorcery or magic.

All natural stones are gifts from heaven. Some individuals not only wear them as jewelry but also carry lucky favorites in a pouch on their person to absorb bad energy or act as a safety measure for added luck. Others incorporate stones into their home decor to add a bit of magic to the environment. It is always advisable to have your favorite stone around as an extra lucky measure. We should learn to take advantage of gemstones' beauty and whatever luck or benefits they offer.

There are little germs all around us that can hold glimmers of inspiration.

—Richelle Mead

Chapter 9

SUPERSTITIONS PRACTICED TO BRING GOOD LUCK

I had only one superstition. I made sure to touch
all the bases when I hit a home run.

—Babe Ruth

Historically, superstitions have been separated into two categories: lucky and unlucky, or good and bad. This outlook most likely stems from a natural acceptance of the superstitions we were taught as children or through word of mouth. As adults, we typically either accept the notion of luck with clear conviction and follow along without thinking twice, or we reject the concept entirely.

I have observed that, for the most part, even those who claim not to be superstitious tread lightly and practice some superstitions; for example, wearing the same article of clothing that you wore when you landed the last business deal to the next venture, or using the same pen time after time on exams, since good grades happen with that particular writing instrument. Perhaps it is all just an attribution theory.

In this chapter, we will review the happy and lucky superstitions. (The scarier ones are discussed in chapter 10.) These positive superstitions are the ones we proudly announce that we carry out in our lives every day. They are beneficial to us, bring some magic into our lives, or help our well-being. The collective thought is, why not employ them? A little good luck never hurt anyone, right?

Below is a list of common lucky charms and other random lucky tidbits.

The Horseshoe
The horseshoe is recognized as a signifier of luck and good fortune. In the past, when blacksmithing was a much-needed trade, horseshoes became a good-luck staple, especially used to guard against the evil witch. Old wives' tales indicate that horses have a keen sense to detect when a witch is in the vicinity. Therefore, a horse would know better than to give a witch a ride. Plus, horses are equipped with horseshoes, a protective metal that can withstand fire. Initially, horseshoes were made of iron. This particular metal was believed to keep away all evil spirits, not just the sorceress. Witches feared horses because they wore this gear; consequently, witches would not bother with horses.

Christians secured horseshoes to houses, barns, and other outbuildings, in an effort to ward off these malevolent females. It was taken a step further by nailing a horseshoe to a loved one's coffin. This ensured protection for the beloved in the afterworld. Sadly, if a woman were suspected of being a witch and died, a horseshoe would be fastened to her casket, signifying she would not be resurrected.

Today, it is a common practice to position a horseshoe on a house or barn door for luck and to ward against evil forces. Some folks place a horseshoe over their beds to prevent bad dreams. Sailors affix a horseshoe to the ship's foremast to ensure smooth sailing and a safe arrival.

It is a good omen to find a horseshoe. Do not give one as a gift, however, as it is deemed unlucky. If you receive one, accept it graciously, and at your first opportunity, bury it in hallowed ground.

Many other societies share in the concept that the horseshoe is a lucky piece. The ancient Greeks, who were a very superstitious society, placed the horseshoe with the ends pointing upward for good luck. What is the proper way to position a horseshoe? Pointed up or pointed down? There is some debate on this. The most popular way seems to be with the ends pointing upward. I agree; I believe the U-shape secures the goodness and blessings surrounding the dwelling without spilling it.

Conversely, some people place the horseshoe in a downward position. Friends of mine believe that is the correct way. Their reasoning? As people enter their home, the horseshoe, with points facing down, will dispose any negativity that a visitor may bring into the house. As a result, it stops any force right at the door. I like that theory. Up or down—which has your vote? There is no right or wrong, since both positions have their merits. It is just a matter of personal opinion.

The Wishbone
The wishbone is a highly regarded superstitious tradition. It involves two people, facing each other and pulling on the turkey's furcula, which is the wishbone. The one who finishes with the longer piece of bone is the winner and is allowed to make one special wish. I have always associated wishbones with Thanksgiving, as the custom is to cook a turkey. As a youngster, I was always excited to ask my mother for the turkey's wishbone. Each year, my brother Gustav and I would pull it together, and we enjoyed ourselves very much.

The tradition of the wishbone dates back to ancient Italy. Italians believed that the goose had magical insight and could predict the future. This bird was seen as a divination tool that could answer many pressing concerns. Women allowed the fowl to choose their future husbands, and the law used them to locate criminals. This ritual was taken very seriously. It was good luck to rub its breastbone as well. The tradition of pulling the furcula of the bird was passed from the Italians to the Romans to the English, and it eventually landed here in the United States, pulling the wishbone of a turkey.

Amulets
An amulet, a word derived from the Latin word *amuletum,* is a good luck charm. This object is worn or carried on the person's body. All cultures have used amulets in all time periods. Its purpose is to ensure personal spiritual protection and safety against bad forces and to provide good luck

to its wearer. A few examples of amulets are gems, coins, pendants, a rabbit's foot, and the Egyptian scarab.

I think that possessing a good luck charm never hurts anyone and might even enhance one's performance, even if the good luck is all in one's mind. For instance, when I was in college, I was convinced that my lucky pen helped me achieve A's on my tests. It gave me more confidence. Since that time, my pen has disappeared. Maybe it knew it had served its purpose.

Rabbit's Foot

A rabbit's foot is one of the more recognized superstitions, yet it's difficult to pinpoint its origin. I have discussed a few possible theories with others concerning how the superstition of rabbit's foot might have begun. For instance, in ancient Europe, certain tribes worshipped animals as protectors. One animal, in particular, was the rabbit. Tribesman would carry pieces, (such as the foot) of the deceased animal, for protection and luck.

Centuries ago, the Celtic culture revered the rabbit as a supernatural being. The Celts believed that because it burrowed beneath the ground, it had a special connection to the gods and whatever else existed sublevel. Celts sought this magic for themselves. They decided that because the foot of a rabbit was the closest body part to the ground, it possessed spiritual power, and therefore, they carried it as a special token of good favor.

Nowadays, it is common to carry a rabbit's foot for good luck—although more controversy arises. Which pocket? The left or the right? A back pocket? This may cause a dilemma. Women tend to throw caution to the wind and attach a rabbit's foot to a handbag or keychain. Today, I feel the tradition is much more liberal but the important aspect is to have the rabbit's foot on your person.

In modern times, using an authentic rabbit's foot is virtually unheard of, unless you are a hunter. I personally like the idea of an artificial bunny's foot, as one of my best childhood buddies was my rabbit, Thumper. Many very cute artificial versions are available. I purchased an adorable, pink faux-fur rabbit's foot for my keychain. Overall, the rabbit's foot represents good fortune to the bearer, no matter its location.

The Scarab Beetle

In ancient Egypt, the scarab was considered extremely sacred. It is depicted in Egyptian artwork. Its likeness was fashioned into various amulets, and this beetle was decidedly the most sacred of all of the Egyptian talismans. It was alleged that honoring the scarab beetle with personalized objects—such as images, stamped stones, carvings, fashioned glass, and beads—would provide the Egyptians the highest level of protection against wicked forces. In addition to Egyptians wearing these tokens while alive, scarab medallions were placed on the hearts of the deceased to protect them on judgment day.

Khepri, the god of the rising sun, was associated with the scarab beetle. Images of this god depict him as having a human body and the head of a beetle. Khepri is known for his great insight, his transformational nature, and his immortality.

I believe that carrying a scarab amulet or wearing scarab jewelry may provide good luck. Years ago, while shopping in a quaint shop in Historic Smithville, New Jersey, I found a scarab bracelet that called to me. I was so excited, as I had been searching for the perfect one. This particular one was a charm bracelet adorned with glass scarabs in various colors. I adored it!

A few years after my purchase, as my husband and I were moving from Pennsylvania to New Jersey, it mysteriously vanished. One would normally deduce I lost the bracelet during all the excitement of the move, but I believe it was under very different circumstances. The following is a true story: our previous home in Pennsylvania, built in the eighteenth century, was a highly active haunted house. In the 1700s, the house was used as a *preparatory home.* Prior to funeral homes, the deceased were laid out at home, but the bodies were prepared for burial elsewhere. Ours was such a place, and when the body was ready, it was placed on our front porch to wait for delivery to the home.

One of our resident ghosts loved jewelry. My husband and I would find old-fashioned pieces of jewelry—clearly not our own—in odd places. Mostly, the jewelry that presented itself, such as a bracelet or ring, was for a small child, although on one occasion I found a gorgeous man's ring. In addition, a few of my items vanished, but the ghosts would always replace them with something else. Maybe the new owners will find my scarab bracelet one day. This is certainly one of life's little mysteries that I love!

Ladybug

I have always held a fascination for the ladybug. She represents peace, happiness, luck, and a window back to my childhood. This delicate and serene bug is member of the beetle family, and I feel she's part of mine as well. The superstitions that surround her cross several cultures, and a few consistent philosophies exist. Here's one: when you find a ladybug, place it on your finger, make a wish, and set it free. She will then fly out into the world to fulfill your wish. Never trap a ladybug in a jar. It's important to handle the ladybug with care and not damage her in any way. Of course, you want your wish fulfilled, but also, it is the humane thing to do.

If the ladybug lands on your hand or arm and flies away herself, it's considered very good luck but also magical. To this day, I enjoy finding a ladybug, making a silent wish, and releasing her into the sky. It is nice when she finds you too.

To simply spot a ladybug guarantees luck, especially in love or finances. Farmers are known to refer to them as the precious beetles sent by the Virgin Mary, as they have appeared in the fields just after praying to the Virgin Mary to protect their crops.

Never, ever kill a ladybug. It is not only cruel, but it results in bad luck.

The Four-Leaf Clover

The four-leaf clover is considered to be the lucky charm of Ireland and has its roots in Christianity. The classic three-leaf clover signifies the Holy Trinity: Father, Son, and Holy Ghost. The fourth leaf of the rarely found four-leaf clover represents the grace of God bestowed on the individual who found it. Furthermore, it brings happiness and a magical shield of safety to those who believe.

My grandmother, a native of Ireland, said that the clover represents happiness overall, but each of the four leaves has a special meaning: love, luck, hope, and faith. Today, the acceptance of the four-leaf clover has evolved beyond Ireland and extends to other parts of the world, especially the United States.

There are many benefits related to finding and keeping a four-leaf clover. One belief is that to hang the clover in the home will ward off evil forces.

Another is to place it in a shoe; then all financial ventures will be prosperous.

If you have a four-leaf clover and give it away, it is said your good luck will be doubled. Because four-leaf clovers are so difficult to find, that would be a very selfless act.

If you wear one as part of a necklace, the clover will allow you to see mystical fairies who prefer to remain invisible.[1]

So many nice choices. Which would you choose?

Four-leaf clovers are rare, but my husband's father, Bill, was a known master at finding them. Purportedly, each and every time Bill would gaze at a field of clover, he would instantly locate a four-leaf clover. This amazed his family, especially my husband, who was with him when he spotted one. Unfortunately, Bill is not among the living any longer, so I cannot witness this with him. I remain constantly on the lookout. No such luck yet, but I keep hoping. Good luck in your four-leaf–clover pursuits.

Pennies
"Pennies from heaven" is an expression indicating that when you find a penny, a relative is communicating from beyond. The deceased is sending well wishes and telling you he or she is fine. The departed realize we are busy with life's details each day, but throwing money in our path will attract attention. That's a smart way to say hello. Whenever I find a penny, I feel it is my father connecting with me. I'd be ecstatic if he dropped a hundred-dollar bill on the ground in front of me; that would be a big greeting!

---

[1] If you are interested in more information on the magical life of the fairy, please read my book *Fairies* (iUniverse 2018).

Random Thoughts about the Lucky Penny

- "Find a penny, pick it up, and all the day you'll have good luck."
- To find a penny in the heads-up position means you will receive extra blessings.
- Spiritually, the number one (the cash value of a penny—one cent) indicates new beginnings and totality. Money has always been related to power, and metal has been linked to attracting wealth and protecting against evil. Thus, the penny is good luck.
- To carry a penny in your pocket will attract money to you. To carry three will triple your chances.
- To place a penny anywhere in your shoe is uncomfortable—but it's lucky.
- On your next cruise, throw a penny into the sea to ensure a safe trip.
- Keeping a glass jar filled with pennies in the kitchen will protect against evil forces.
- When gifting a wallet or handbag, place a penny inside so the new owner receives good luck.
- If you experience a troublesome issue, throw a penny away from you. It will take your cares with it.
- To ensure your wish will come true, toss a penny over your shoulder, not directly into the fountain.
- Pennies with holes carry extra luck.

The Number Seven

Throughout history, various societies and religions have been in agreement that seven is a blessed number, and many superstitions have stemmed from it. Centuries ago, seven was a popular number because only seven planets were known to exist. Furthermore, ancient Rome and Egypt regarded this number as very important and based their customs around it. The early Romans and Egyptians had seven gods. The ancient Greeks, Romans, and Egyptians thought of seven as the ultimate perfect number.

The Bible perceives seven as a flawless number. In the New Testament of the Christian Bible, many instances relating to the number seven are evident: seven seals in the book of Revelation, seven heavenly virtues, seven stars, seven deadly sins, the seven last plagues, and, in Catholicism, the seven sacraments. In the Old Testament, the number seven is mentioned multiple times and is believed to be a stamp of God's work. For instance, God dictated the seventh day as a day of rest after his creation took six days to complete. The Hebrew Torah suggests that a holy year arises every seven years, and sitting shiva (a word that means "seven") is to mourn a deceased person for seven days. Indeed, seven is a magical number.

Seven doesn't end there, though. The human body has seven energy centers called chakras. Written music is based on seven basic notes. Blacksmiths once fashioned horseshoes with seven nails. Modern-day gamblers hope to see the number seven displayed across a slot-machine screen, and they pray for three number-seven cards while playing blackjack. They also hope for sevens while playing craps and claim that if dice are rolled twice, the probability of getting a seven in combination is greater than any other combination.

The beat goes on. Listed below are arbitrary tidbits concerning the number seven.

- A rainbow possesses seven colors: red, orange, yellow, green, blue, indigo, and violet.
- The *Harry Potter* series is composed of seven books.
- The ladybug has seven spots.
- There are seven seas: the Arctic, North Atlantic, South Atlantic, North Pacific, South Pacific, Indian, and Southern Oceans (modern seven seas).
- There are seven continents: North America, South America, Africa, Antarctica, Australia, Asia, and Europe.
- The seven wonders of the ancient world are Colossus of Rhodes, Great Pyramid of Giza, Hanging Gardens of Babylon, the Lighthouse of Alexandria, Mausoleum at Halicarnassus, Temple of Artemis, and the Statue of Zeus at Olympia.
- The seven sister states in northeastern India line the neighboring states of Arunachal Pradesh, Assam, Meghalaya, Manipur, Mizoram, Nagaland, and Tripura.
- "The seven-year itch" is marital expression to indicate that after the seven-year mark in one's marriage, a decline in happiness results. A well-known movie starring Marilyn Monroe, *The Seven-Year*

Itch, was a romantic comedy that popularized the expression a bit more.

- The Seven Dwarfs are Grumpy, Doc, Bashful, Happy, Sneezy, Dopey, and Sleepy. Interestingly, these names belong to the Disney version. The Brothers Grimm tale used different names.
- Seven days comprise a calendar week.
- Shakespeare's seven ages of man are infant, schoolboy, lover, soldier, justice, Pantalone, and old age.
- "All the world's a stage" is a phrase coined by William Shakespeare and begins a monologue from William in *As You Like It*, act II, scene VII, in which he offers the analogy of the world being a stage and life its stage.
- The seven deadly sins are avarice, envy, gluttony, lust, pride, sloth and wrath.
- Seven years of bad luck follow breaking a mirror.
- I know of seven couples who were married on July 7, 2007, or 7/7/07.
- Have you heard the old joke, Why is 10 afraid of 7? Because 7, 8 (ate) 9!

Salt

Salt is revered as very lucky and powerful. (It may also have unlucky connotations, as you will read in chapter 10.) This white crystalline substance is considered as much more than a spice used to enhance the taste of food. Salt is helpful in spiritual matters. When placed in a bath, after a soak, a person will feel spiritually cleansed. The salt releases toxins and lifts negativity away from the body.[2]

In addition, when salt is placed in the corners of a house, it will keep the home safe and deter lurking evil spirits. Some old-timers believe that bad spirits are drawn to new construction and plan to wreak havoc on the new owners. It sounds far-fetched, but some home builders with means have employed temporary residents to live in the house first in order to deal with the demons before their own arrival.

---

[2] For more information on the use of salt for cleansing purposes, please consult my book, *Passport to Heaven's Angelic Messages* (iUniverse 2016).

Full Moon

The full moon has been considered magical for centuries and is surrounded by various superstitions, both good and bad. The earth experiences a full lunar phase of the moon about every twenty-nine days. This occurs when the moon is completely on the opposite end of the sun. Therefore, the earth views the moon as appearing completely illuminated, or full.

I encourage you to take advantage of the time when the moon is completely full. Because this is a mystical time, it is wise to charge crystals under the moonlight to cleanse them. If you are a new parent, exposing your newborn to the full moon's light for a few seconds will bestow good luck and strength. Wishes are said to come true when the request is made while facing the full moon.

Spitting

Believe it or not, for centuries, spit has been viewed as a great tool to guard against evil. Spittle is an alternative way of anointing and blessing others with good luck. For instance, fisherman and sailors spit on or over the top of their boats for luck to ensure a successful sail and bountiful catch. Children spit on marbles to win the game. Fighters spit on their knuckles before a fight to produce powerful punches. Gamblers spit on the cash before betting. Some people have been known to spit in their hands before a large physical undertaking. Ignore the germ factor, and give this a whirl.

Saint Joseph

Trying to sell your home? Need a little assistance? Call Joseph, the Catholic saint, to the rescue. Saint Joseph is the adoptive father of Jesus and husband to Mother Mary. He was a carpenter by trade, considered the provider of the household, and in charge of the caring for the dwelling space of the holy family. Hence, Saint Joseph is connected with the care of the home and its occupants. Today, religious stores sell a small statue of Joseph so that he will expedite the sale.

How does the Saint Joseph statue work? You don't have to be a Catholic to ask for his assistance. In fact, some Catholics believe it should be forbidden, as it goes against Catholicism. Below are my tips:

Purchase a Saint Joseph statue (typically made of plastic or resin) or the "Home Sale" kit, which includes the statue and instructions regarding the prayers and actions involved. You can order it online or buy one at a Catholic store. (As a shop owner told me as I was buying mine, Saint Joseph practically flies off the shelf in a bad real estate market.) The kit comes with both literature and the statue.

Or you may decide to only select the statue, read my instructions, and pray for Saint Joseph's intercession by reciting your own prayer.

Methods of burying the statue vary. You have the following choices:

- Bury the statue in the ground a few inches into the earth, either head up or upside down (your choice), next to the For Sale sign. (I felt uncomfortable about placing Saint Joseph downward on his head.) It may be facing the house or the road, whichever is your preference. Facing inward indicates buyers will come in. Facing outward means you will sell and leave the residence.
- Place the statue in the interior front of the house near the door, facing outward away toward the street.
- Situate the figurine in the ground, two to three feet from the rear of the house, upside down, facing away from the home. Please bury deep enough to ensure that later, a lawn mower won't destroy it.
- If selling a condominium or you are not interested in situating Saint Joseph in the ground, place him in a flowerpot located by the front door.

Once the house has sold, the statue should be recovered and then placed in an area of respect and gratitude in the new home. In the event you don't recall where Joseph was positioned in the ground or the time of year does not allow unearthing the statue, a similar statue may be purchased to sit in the new home.

I have sought the aid of Saint Joseph. A few years ago, we relocated from Pennsylvania to New Jersey. At first, my husband and I were interested in moving but weren't technically looking or ready to put our current home up for sale. However, one day, we accidently stumbled upon our new home, and it spoke to me. As we were walking toward the river, I saw a For Sale sign and quickly declared to my husband, "I want it."

From that moment, we were in an incredible rush to ready and ultimately sell our existing home to move to New Jersey. The fall season was becoming winter, and some real estate agents claimed it was tougher to sell with the holidays approaching and school already in session.

I rushed to a Catholic store, bought a Saint Joseph house kit, and prayed that he would work immediately. I buried him, head up, facing the house, near the For Sale sign. Also, I placed another of the same type of statue in our front window, facing out, to make my odds greater. Thank you, Saint Joseph! We received an offer within two months of the listing and on a date very close to Christmas. Before moving, I tried to unearth the statue, but the ground was frozen solid. He remained. I apologized to Saint Joseph, and I'm sure he understood that the weather conditions made it impossible to retrieve him. Since I had purchased a second statue, I arranged that one in a prominent location in the new residence as a thank you, where it remains today. The couple who bought our house in Pennsylvania were ecstatic, so it was a win/win. If you are in the market to sell, try my suggestion. I wish you good luck for an expedient and successful sale.

God Bless—The Sneezing Superstition
Various superstitions surround sneezing. A sneeze may be annoying, but it does have positive benefits, as it cleanses the sinus cavity. While a sneeze to Americans is usually just a sneeze, in other parts of the world, it may be considered a bad sign or even a warning. However, since ancient times, good tidings have surrounded the sneeze.

The widespread expression, "God bless you," or simply, "Bless you" has roots in the fifteenth century. At that time, the bubonic plague wiped out many citizens throughout Europe. One symptom of the plague was a strong and frequent sneeze. Many felt death would follow the sneeze. The religious power at that time, Pope Gregory the Great, ruled that those who sneezed should be blessed straightaway with holy words. This consecration would protect them from certain immediate death. It was believed that to sneeze into a cloth would be to try to contain the soul in the body. Others professed the sneeze expelled a demon, and the hope was this blessing would purify that individual promptly.

My family believes in uttering the German word *gesundheit* immediately following a sneeze, as it wishes the sneezer good health. Until recently, I thought everyone communicated some form of "bless you" to one another. I didn't realize that the religion of Jehovah's Witnesses does not follow that tradition. According to Marcus Escritos in "10 Things That Sucked about Growing Up a Jehovah's Witness" (2014), "Jehovah's Witnesses don't say 'god bless you' when someone sneezes, because that practice supposedly has a pagan origin."

Random Lucky Practices

Finally, below is a quick list of random lucky superstitions:

- Itchy palm? Right or left? If the right palm itches, money is coming. Conversely, if the left palm itches, money will be lost through gambling, bad investments, or an unexpected bill, or cash will be dropped accidentally. Naturally, my itching always seems to affect the left palm. The other day, as I was purchasing a lottery ticket, the customer next to me mentioned her palm had been itching for days, which led her to believe she was about to win cash. I asked if it was the right or left palm. She replied it was her right palm, the lucky one. A superstitious person—I love to hear it!
- Itchy nose? An itchy nose forecasts a sweet kiss is on the way. It may also mean you will encounter an argument.
- A quick sneeze indicates a person very far away misses you.
- Rice tossed at a newly married couple increases the odds for many children.
- The seventh child of the seventh child will be psychically gifted.
- If you dream about a white cat, you will have good luck.
- Sudden and short ringing in the ear indicates someone is speaking kindly about you.
- Garlic hung in the home offers spiritual protection.
- Sugar placed in a cup prior to pouring tea into it will bring happiness.
- To step on your own shadow evokes good luck.

- To throw a shoe at a friend or relative as he or she is leaving for a trip invites good luck.
- Eating green candy is extremely lucky.
- Present a newly married couple with clover for a happy, long, life together.
- Give a dime to a new car owner, who should be instructed to place it under the driver's mat for luck and safety.
- Always carry a dollar in your wallet, but never spend it. This attracts more money.
- Hold your breath as you pass by a cemetery. The belief is that a trapped soul will be released to heaven. My sister, Megan, and I would try this when we were riding in the car together. On one occasion, the cemetery was so long that I couldn't hold my breath the entire way across, but Megan did. Thanks to Megan, a trapped soul was freed. (Thankfully, neither of us was driving.)
- Lucky colors: red is the color of blood or life and will bring happiness, wealth, fame, and good luck. White is the color of mother's milk. It symbolizes moderation, purity, honesty, life, and balance.
- Knocking on wood is an old Christian practice. Jesus's cross was fashioned of wood; therefore, to knock on a piece of wood offers magical results, especially to keep evil forces at bay after a positive statement is spoken. For example, a person may say in conversation, "I have never gotten a traffic ticket," and immediately follow up by knocking on a piece of wood, such as a wooden chair or door. This ensures that he or she will not be jinxed by the comment.
- Crossing one's fingers is another superstition that stems from the Christian faith. Similar to knocking on wood as a positive statement is spoken, he or she crosses fingers and holds them up in the air. This deters evil spirits from ruining any chance of good fortune.
- Have you ever received a bird dropping on your outfit or hair as you were walking? One would think this would be incredibly bad luck, but it is considered good luck. One afternoon while strolling across a walking bridge, I was lucky enough to get a big mess in my hair. Lucky me.

- To fasten a safety pin somewhere on your outfit prior to a journey will ensure safe travels. The metal acts as a protector.
- Twelve is considered the complete, whole, and perfect number. Several reasons exist as to why this is the thought. The zodiac has a total of twelve signs; twelve months are in a year; the day is considered to be divided into twelve-hour increments as day and night.

Good luck charms, such as an amulet worn around the neck or a rabbit's foot tucked in one's pocket, is a safeguard. It is a good feeling to know we may rely on different beliefs, rituals, and helpful trinkets to make life safer, easier, and lucky. Why risk lack of spiritual protection or good fortune by not taking such easy precautions? My theory is that when enough people believe in a particular superstition, a certain amount of positive power is released into the universe. If a good luck charm offers a form of protection or emotional well-being, why not use it? A little good luck and assistance is always welcome!

I have a terrible superstition of writing things down.

—Andrew Scott

Chapter 10

Superstitions Practiced to Prevent Bad Luck

Superstition is the irrational belief that an object or behavior has the power to influence an outcome, where there is no logical connection between them. Most of us aren't superstitious, but most of us are "littlestitious."

—Gretchen Rubin

Do you dare to enter the unlucky arena of superstition? I urge you to take the journey. It will be not only eerily fun but informative. You will acquire the knowledge of what to beware of and, in some cases, the cautionary steps to lessen or counteract any possible ill effects. Please pay close attention, for your own safety and peace of mind, to a few unlucky superstitions regarding umbrellas, shoes, poles, and handbags, and why sneezing and table salt may also be unlucky as well as many other unlucky tidbits.

Umbrella
The superstition of the umbrella holds that it is unlucky to open one indoors. I feared this until I learned the reasoning behind this belief. In Victorian England, females carried umbrellas to protect their skin from the sun. The sunshades of that period were not designed as safely as umbrellas are today.

Then, metal hinges proved unsafe, and on occasion, the umbrella would pop open indoors. This malfunction proved to be most dangerous when the umbrella propelled like a rocket through the air in the home. Children or anyone in its path could be injured, mirrors broken (doubly unlucky), and furniture damaged. This led to the belief that opening an umbrella inside was not only hazardous but unlucky.

Today, we don't open an umbrella inside since it is viewed as bad luck. The reason, however, is not only because of the parasols of yesteryear but on the rain umbrellas carried by men in 1700s London. During that period, men carried large and dangerously constructed umbrellas, made with heavy metal spokes. These were equally risky to pop open indoors, also causing injuries to those in the surrounding area.

In ancient Egypt, it was considered unfortunate to open an umbrella indoors for different reasons. The shade beneath was seen as a sacred space, and anyone who encroached on that space brought bad luck to themselves and the umbrella's owner. At that time, umbrellas were used as protection from the excessive heat, sun, and especially malevolent spirits. Only citizens with high-status positions, such as religious leaders or aristocrats, possessed umbrellas. It was frowned upon to open an umbrella indoors, as that would offend the son goddess. She protected the sky, much as an umbrella enveloped a civilian with security. In order to pay this goddess homage, umbrellas were fashioned in her honor and adorned with pretty peacock feathers. Again, these were reserved for upper-class or recognized people.

Shoes

The superstition concerning shoes warns to never place a pair on the table. This was a hot topic in my house when I was a small child. After a shopping trip, none of us was allowed to place his or her new shoes on the table—or at any point, for that matter—for my mother warned it was unlucky, as well as unsanitary. Even as a child, I was not interested in resting my shoes on the kitchen or dining room table, especially since my family calls me a germ freak.

A few centuries ago, the dinner table in one's home was a popular place to dress a corpse for burial. Once outfitted, his or her shoes were placed on top of the corpse's chest, not on the feet. Footwear positioned directly on the table top equated to the spirit not entering heaven or even another death in the home. Theater folks refrain from putting shoes on the dressing room table, as it is believed the show might suffer. It's no wonder my mother was adamant about this belief.

Sneezing

In chapter 9, I discussed that sneezing might be a lucky act, but there are always two sides to a story. Old wives' tales say the downside to a sneeze is that it foretells death. Centuries ago, people thought this head blast would surely kill the person who sneezed or another nearby. It wasn't understood that a sneeze was provoked by an irritation in the nasal cavity. The reality is that individuals sneeze every day; unfortunately, individuals die each day as well but not because of the sneeze. Those are facts, but the two are unrelated. One thing is for sure: we all have a 100 percent chance of dying one day.

I conducted research and found that in 2017, the number of deaths in the United States, according to the National Vital Statistics System, was 2,813,503. On a happier note, Linda Searing wrote in an article for the *Washington Post* (2018), "The Big Number: 3.8 million babies were born in the U.S. last year. That's a drop. Last year, 3,853,472 babies were born in the United States."

Even though the number of babies born has dropped since 2016, 1,039,969 more souls were born than died that year.

As an eerie aside, there is a website that lists the current mortality rate, birth rate, and other statistics. It is live, so the numbers are ever changing in front of your eyes. As I was writing this chapter on April 25, 2019, at 3:06 p.m. ET, there were 18,540,480 deaths and 44,189,480 births worldwide for the year. As you are reading this, I'm sure it has escalated. Try this website for yourself: https://www.worldometers.info.

Salt

Spilling salt is not a favored practice. In ancient Rome and Egypt, salt was a very valuable commodity, and in the Middle Ages, it was used for medicinal purposes. Spillage was to be avoided at all costs and was viewed as a very unlucky practice. In biblical days, Judas, the apostle who betrayed Jesus, spilled salt during the Last Supper, and that gave the practice a negative connotation.

In the event that you spill salt, you should instantly pick some of it up and throw it over your left shoulder to negate any bad luck caused by the spill. This practice was begun by the ancient Egyptians and Romans. In contemporary times, the price of salt has come down a great deal.

Full Moon

As I've mentioned, the full moon has a few negative beliefs surrounding it. As a child, I was fearful of a full moon shining through my window and onto my bed. I was told people might go crazy from sleeping in moonlight. Years later, a researcher friend told me there is no scientific evidence to substantiate that claim, and there is no correlation between human behavior and the full moon. Yet superstition does not take science into account.

Friends of mine in the police field and those who work in emergency room positions think more individuals demonstrate unstable behavior during a full moon than during other phases of the moon. You may have heard people remark that there must be a full moon because a coworker or relative is acting off-kilter.

A few other full-moon superstitions to beware of include the following:

- Noticing the moon over one's left shoulder brings bad luck.
- Camping under the full moon (without a tent) is an unlucky omen.
- Beware of swimming in the ocean during a full moon, as the beings in the sea may act strangely or aggressively.

Poles

Have you heard the expression "Do not split a pole"? According to urbandictionary.com,

> Splitting pole is considered bad luck by some people.
> When walking in a group and obstructed by an obstacle,
> i.e. a pole, traffic cone, whatever it is, it is important for

those who believe in this superstition that the group does not separate on either side of this obstacle.

This is one superstition my family never mentioned to me, but a coworker recently introduced it to me. As she and I were strolling on our break, casually talking, she suddenly interjected forcefully, "Do not split the pole." I was taken aback but was intrigued and compelled to ask what this meant. Since there are many poles in the small city in which we work and walk, the probability of it happening is great. I'm sure I did this many times prior to her warning. (Is ignorance bliss?)

For fun, when I returned to work, I asked a coworker if she was superstitious, and if so, which superstitious belief she considered number one. I never expected such an immediate and hearty response! "Splitting a pole," she answered.

Beware! In the future, whether you're walking with a group or just one person, please stay on the same side of the pole. In the event you cannot, murmur the phrase, "Bread and butter." This negates any ill effects that splitting a pole may bring.

Handbags
Have you heard the expression, "A purse on the floor is money out the door"? This was another superstition unfamiliar to me until one day my hair stylist noticed that I had placed my bag on the floor. She cautioned me never to do that again, as I would always be broke. That explained my finances. Unknowingly, I had done this for years, which is shocking to me, as I'm such a germ freak. The next time I went to the salon, I saw that my stylist had placed a handbag hook at her station.

Why is a dim view taken of leaving one's handbag on the floor? One reason is feng shui, which originated in China. Feng shui is the science of placing objects in favorable locations to create a positive flow of energy. It is believed that placing your bag on the floor is improper.

I suspect another reason could be that potential thieves, especially during the holiday season, are lurking and waiting for an unsuspecting person to leave a handbag on the ground. Typically, not only cash but credit cards are stolen. This not only means money out the door but possibly an individual's identity as well.

Threes

The expression "It comes in threes" predicts that death will arrive in groups of three. The theory is that if there is one death, two more will quickly follow in a particular group, such as work, family, celebrity deaths, and so on. Over the years, I have found this has expanded to any unfortunate occurrence arriving three at a time and within a short time span.

In an article by John Allen Paulos, "Bad Things in Threes? It Doesn't Add Up" (2009), he suggests it is still a popular belief today. Paulos writes,

> Michael Jackson's untimely death coupled with the deaths of Ed McMahon and Farrah Fawcett in the same week revived the belief of many that celebrity deaths, plane crashes and all manner of catastrophes come in threes.

In my opinion, this is a sad superstition. I remember talk of it when an acquaintance suffered a death in his family. After his uncle passed away, he mentioned the other members in his family began to eyeball each other, wondering who would be next. That's very uncomfortable. I don't know how it concluded.

Not to add to the misery, but three knocks on the door of the room of a dying person hurries his or her death. Next time you visit a close-to-death individual, beware of rapping three times to announce your visit.

Step on a Crack; Break Your Mother's Back

This is a nasty expression. In times past, mothers and fathers used this expression as a scare tactic to ensure that their children listened and behaved. Parents also have told their children the following:

- The number of cracks a kid steps on will be the actual number of bones the child's mother will break, in her back or elsewhere.

- If a child doesn't avoid cracks, a mean bear will hop out of the woods and eat the child.
- Never step on a crack because evil monsters live inside. If so, monsters will appear at bedtime, when the child is all alone, and torment him or her.

There are so many variables connected with this expression. Some sidewalks are full of cracks. How could anyone be 100 percent certain of not stepping on a crack? Why would parents think the threat of this expression would make a child comply with all parental rules? When I was a child, during recess on the playground, the boys threw all caution to the wind and jumped on cracks.

Random Unlucky Practices
The following collection of unfortunate and somewhat eerie superstitions are something for you to ponder. Remember, don't tempt fate, as they purportedly deliver bad luck.

- Crossing one's eyes may make them stay that way.
- Never give your baby a haircut prior to his or her first birthday. If you do, he or she will forever deal with unruly hair.
- If your ears suddenly begin to ring, another is speaking badly about you.
- Do not gift a pair of shoes to your spouse or significant other, for he or she will one day wear those shoes to walk right out of your life.
- Hold on to that dishcloth. If one is dropped, bad luck is on the way.
- To eat directly from a hot pot will cause it to rain at the next wedding ceremony attended. Please don't ruin anyone's upcoming nuptials.
- It is a bad omen to spit at an owl in broad daylight.
- To dream of an unknown black dog means enemies are conspiring against you.
- Always get out of bed on the same side—or else!
- If you sleep with your feet toward the door, an unkind ghost may try to steal your soul.
- If you whistle outdoors at night, a nightwalker may follow you home.

- When a cat sneezes three times indoors, it will rain within the next twenty-four hours.
- If an owl hoots in your garden, the crops will die.
- To place a hat on the bed is unlucky.
- A death is forthcoming if a mirror falls from the wall and shatters. (I can attest to this one.)
- Do not comb your hair if you have friends or relatives taking a cruise, for they will become very seasick. You will suffer messy hair until their return.
- A framed photo that falls from the wall and breaks foretells a money loss.
- Please remove your hat and respect a funeral procession or the dead may haunt you.
- Do not rock an empty chair with your hand, count the number of cars in a funeral procession, or walk through a cemetery with a newborn, or general bad luck will follow.
- To bury a woman in black or to wear black to her funeral means she will haunt you.
- After leaving a funeral home, never proceed directly home, or ghosts of the dead will follow.
- Ghosts appear to those who gaze into a mirror by candlelight.
- Do not place the master suite above the garage or the marriage will be full of woe. My mother doesn't follow this superstition. In fact, after my parents were married, they built a lovely home, and their master bedroom suite was located over the garage. They were happily married for over fifty years.

It is true that many unlucky superstitions exist, but there is one overall commonality. Our aim is to attract good luck and avoid bad luck. Happily, there are remedies to some of the unlucky traditions, which may lessen the worry surrounding them. For instance, after making a certain statement about good fortune or happy plans, knocking on wood may alleviate some tension. It's believed that knocking on wood will chase away the evil spirits who may prey on the boastful person.

If you catch yourself stressing, keep in mind that most beliefs have been passed down through the centuries and often have become embellished— sometimes to the point of being frightening. Some become rooted in our minds, and those are difficult to dismiss, especially the ones we were taught as children. However, just take a step back, and use your own judgment. We cannot adhere to each and every one, nor should we do so.

In my opinion, luck is very much like manifestation—keeping a positive or negative attitude will draw those intentions toward you. The mind is a powerful tool that can create what you believe, either good or bad. The next time a mirror breaks, you split a pole, or are face-to-face with another chilling superstition, remember you are in control. You have free will and may accept or reject the superstition. You have the power.

Security is mostly a superstition. It does not exist in nature, nor do the children of men as a whole experience it. Avoiding danger is no safer in the long run than outright exposure. Life is either a daring adventure or nothing.

—Helen Keller

Chapter 11

SUPERSTITION: MEN VERSUS WOMEN

Science is the great antidote to the poison of enthusiasm and superstition.

—Adam Smith

Does a sincere disparity exist between the views of men and women regarding superstition? Do males and females differ strongly in their beliefs? I have concluded the answer is yes. Although my husband, John, and his associates insist that the level of superstitious belief depends on educational level, I have not found that to be true. Personally, I have always believed that the amount of one's belief is based on gender. Following that particular discussion with John, I decided to add a section based on my own study. In this chapter, I will provide the findings from my study, which proved there is a gap between men and women with regard to superstition. Enjoy the results from my handcrafted survey, as well other certain superstitions among the non-skeptics polled.

The Male versus Female Study
My sampling consisted of one hundred people; fifty males and fifty females, ranging in age from fifteen to ninety-one. Their annual incomes ranged from zero dollars to $150,000. The education level ranged from a high

school student to PhD level, and their job titles were diverse. Titles included Reiki professional, business owner, day care associate, investigator, landscaper, project developer, prison guard, pilot, domestic engineer, and retired teacher. This random sampling engaged participants who reside in the United States, yet lived in areas spanning from the East Coast to the Midwest to the West Coast, in California.

Each participant was asked his or her age, gender, education level, job title, salary, and state of residence as well as the following two questions:

- Are you superstitious?
- If so, what is your strongest superstitious belief?

Results
This particular survey demonstrated, by a large number, that females are more superstitious than males. The findings reflected an odd juxtaposition; of the fifty men questioned, *only four believed* in superstition. Conversely, of the fifty women, *four did* not *believe* in superstition. According to my study, the results coincide nicely with my theory—that superstition is based on gender. Furthermore, it did not point to any correlation between education level, work title, salary, age, or location.

Metrics
The findings were incongruent, yet ironically, the opposite mirror image of one another.

Males

- 8 percent (4 of 50 surveyed) believe in superstition.
- 92 percent (46 of 50 surveyed) do not believe in superstition.

Females

- 92 percent (4 of 50 surveyed) believe in superstition.
- 8 percent (4 of 50 surveyed) do not believe in superstition.

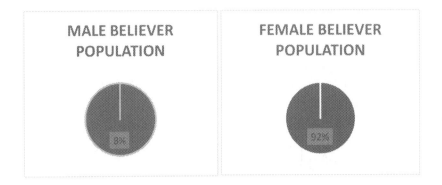

MALE BELIEVER POPULATION — 8%

FEMALE BELIEVER POPULATION — 92%

It is important to note that in this study, the four men considered themselves serious advocates. The majority of the women were emphatic in their beliefs, while only a handful seemed to be on the fence, deciding they were more superstitious than not.

The Men's Personal Superstitions

Two men said they felt it necessary to wear a lucky garment to an important event. Each stated his particular item brings good luck, and both could not do without it. One elaborated, saying that when dressing, he must place his attire on in the same order each and every time or it would not be lucky. The other said that if he positions his baseball cap on his head backward before a ball game, it ensures his team will win.

One gentleman polled was dead serious with his answer about his personal superstition, although I'm not sure if he was teasing me. Since I cannot skew the results with my own view and must accept their statements and base my final conclusion on them, he was counted into the believer group. You may draw your own conclusion. This man explained that his individual superstition is to drink a very potent alcoholic beverage called Devil's Juice prior to any speaking engagement. He said it provides him with fortuity, confidence, and good results, each and every time.

I have never tried that powerful concoction and never will because of its reputation. If I were committed to speak in public, drinking even a sip of Devil's Juice would destroy any speech I planned to present, and I would appear very foolish to the audience. To my understanding, this very intoxicating beverage is nothing to fool with, and I don't suggest or condone that you try it for yourself.

Male preferences are as follows:

- wearing a lucky item prior to attending an important event
- subscribing to a personal superstition

The Women's Personal Superstitions
The favorite superstitions among the female population, ranked from highest to lowest in popularity, are as follows:

- spilling salt
- splitting a pole
- finding a penny
- opening an umbrella indoors
- miscellaneous common traditions
- belief in a personally concocted superstition

Random individual beliefs provided by the polled superstitious females are as follows:

- Be kind and happy on New Year's Day.
- Don't get a haircut during a full moon.
- Each day, it is necessary to drive past a lucky tree.
- Never wear the color green—ever.
- Get into bed only when the clock reads one minute after the hour.
- If you see an owl, hoot at it.
- If you see a man wearing green at midnight, do not make eye contact with him.
- Only drive into a major city on the thirteenth of the month.
- Plant a bush in your backyard to celebrate a happy event.
- If you see a ghost in the middle of the night, look out the window.
- Do not keep mirrors in the bedroom facing the bed.

It was my true pleasure to poll, interact with, and learn of the different views from the folks who were surveyed. My eternal thanks to each one of them.

Are you wondering what my highest-rated superstitious belief is? I do subscribe to a boatload, but my number one is that *bad news comes in threes*. Since I have been introduced to new superstitions through this study, I now have more to worry about. Believing can become exhausting.

As I concluded, men appear to be more impervious than women to superstition. However, the media portrays them differently. For instance, commercials feature males as a superstitious gender. Are these ads written by women? An advertisement during Super Bowl season shows a man's comfy chair placed on the curb for trash day. The man is then shown inside the house, watching football but seemingly bothered. Next, he places his chair back inside the house. The viewer is lead to believe that was his lucky chair.

Another example: on the popular television show *Blue Bloods*, the ever-so-serious New York City police commissioner Frank Reagan, played by Tom Selleck, is a superstitious person. In season six, episode twelve, titled "Cursed," Commissioner Reagan displays strong feelings that a particular badge number is cursed. The badge number 46808 once belonged to the commissioner's son, Joe, who was killed on duty. Other instances of the numbers 468 and 4680 make the commissioner very apprehensive. During a discussion with his father, Henry Reagan (played Len Cariou), Henry admits he has carried a lucky silver dollar with him for years. Hmmm ... a man admitting he believes in superstition. This is very rare and may blow my theory.

Back to the story ... The reason this is a hot topic for Frank Reagan is that another officer has asked permission to use this badge number. It has sentimental value to a female police officer, Jill Carpenter, as it was her father's number when he was a cop in Boston. Later in the show, during the traditional Reagan Sunday dinner, Frank poses the question of whether to release the badge number. The entire family discusses it, even the younger children, and after much debate, the verdict is yes. Later on,

Officer Carpenter is shot. This confirms Frank's superstition, and he is beside himself, thinking this badge number was indeed cursed.

Frank makes a hospital visit to Jill and learns that at the time of the shooting, Jill was not wearing the shield number. Whew, a relief! Frank was calmed but believed if she had been, it would have been curtains for Officer Jill Carpenter. I'm surprised Frank didn't believe, since she was shot just being associated with the number.

One day, my wish is to play a cousin from New Jersey, who is in town briefly and invited to the Reagan Sunday gathering. Please seat me between Frank and Danny. I swear I will not blab any of the confidential information shared during dinner. Everyone has a dream bucket list, right? I just adore the show *Blue Bloods* and suggest that you give this crime/drama series a try if you haven't already. I'm sure you will get hooked!

How Much Superstition in a Single Day?
Recently, for amusement, I decided to choose a random weekday to conduct another study. This time, my goal was to calculate the number of times in one day I noticed some form of superstition being mentioned or practiced. My criteria were overhearing a conversation in any location (in the workplace, at the store, through media, etc.) or witnessing a random act. I was determined not to look for superstition practices but rather to simply observe what came my attention.

In one day, I observed the following:

- In the morning, outside my office, one female said to another female, "I don't want to jinx myself but ..."
- Later that morning, during a meeting, one female said to another, "I'm stuck with the unlucky chair."
- Toward lunchtime, a female was explaining to anyone who would listen that she notices that when she verbally states or mentally thinks about an object she likes or partakes in something she especially enjoys, the item suddenly breaks, or the enjoyment is taken away. Now, she feels superstitious and will not mention anything she loves any longer. This young woman provided examples. She loved her curling iron but the style has been

discontinued. The very next day, it broke. One day, she thought how much she loved to walk along the wooded path in her town each day after work. Shortly after, it was fenced off indefinitely and became inaccessible.

- At the end of the day, on the elevator, one woman said to another, "I don't want to curse you, but it seems like your ex has been leaving you alone."
- During my drive home, I saw a bumper sticker that read, "Luck is what you make it." I did not notice the gender of the driver.
- Early that evening, my mother called me to report she'd just won on five scratch-off lottery tickets. Her lucky number is five because she has five children.
- Later that evening, the host of a popular game show us the word "lucky."

Today, take a moment to notice how often the people in your life and the media reference superstition. You will be amazed at your findings!

As I was creating this chapter, I penned a silly little poem with regard to my perception of the views of males and females in general:

I definitely find men and women have a different way of looking at things.
I suppose that can be one spice that life brings.
It can be amusing to listen to the male perspective, and sometimes it seems like a bunch of baloney.
Yet I choose to listen politely because my name is Toni.

Each one of us is entitled to his or own opinion, and this makes life interesting. Generally, in the realm of superstition, it does appear that women tend to be hard-wired for superstition, while men describe themselves as following the path of rational and scientific thinking. In my experience, women are recognized as empathic individuals who are more likely to be open to, discuss, and share views and opinions on their supernatural philosophies more causally than their male counterparts. Although my objective was to prove my personal theory that the male and female viewpoints vary on superstition, of course other variables do contribute to some degree—cultural views, age, upbringing, ancestry, and religious background, to name a few. All taken together, this creates an interesting mix of ingredients.

There is a fifth dimension, beyond that which is known to man. It is a dimension as vast as space and timeless as infinity. It is the middle ground between light and shadow, between science and superstition.

—Rod Serling

AUTHOR'S NOTE

Thank you for selecting *Are You Superstitious?* I hope you delighted in reading of our world steeped in superstition as much as I enjoyed sharing my knowledge and research. At times, superstition can be a wee bit intimidating. Perhaps, in a strange way, it may act as an alarm to warn us against being overconfident at times when we should err on the side of caution or being confident in those situations when we need assistance. Either way, it is exciting to exist in a world that holds such mystery. The key is to have fun and not take any of it too literally. The world of superstition is here to stay no matter what the cynics think. To me, that's good news. Remember, we all have the power to make our own luck.

If you found *Are you Superstitious?* a pleasurable read, please consider another one of my books. Do you have an interest in angels, fairies, or both? My first guide, *Passport to Heaven's Angelic Messages*, will direct you on the ways to recognize, receive, and decipher your own personal communication from the divine. If you enjoy the fairy realm and would like to know more about these beings, read my second published work, *Fairies.* You will learn about the different types of fairies, why they exist on earth, the ways to acquaint yourself with the fairy realm, a lesson in fairy craft making, hosting an enchanted party, and much more. *Ian Greets The World* is a children's book featuring a boy named Ian who teaches the way to say "hello" as he travels to eight countries and stops at the famous landmark which is unique to that particular country. No passport needed!

I'd love to hear from you! Feel free to communicate with me via email, toniklein@ymail.com, or on Facebook: Toni Klein Author.

THIRTEEN TALES OF SUPERSTITION

I am finicky about making sure my sneakers are pretty tight. It is almost like a superstition to me.

—John McEnroe

I find it fascinating that our world is bursting with faith in the unknown. Personally, I'm thrilled. This section offers a collection of short stories and quotes contributed by individuals with diverse life experiences and perspectives. Yet, very interestingly, a commonality of views and belief in the realm of superstition exists among them.

Beneath find *thirteen* accounts for your reading pleasure. The first three are experiences which pertain to my life.

Enjoy!

There are certain ways to beat the curse of the evil eye-if one is prepared. Of course, anyone is susceptible to getting it at any time from anyone. An alarming way to think, but realistic. A year ago, a friend introduced me to her Aunt, Nora. She was a fanatic with reference to the curse of the evil eye and was never seen without her cornicello. Aunt Nora, as she liked to be addressed, would advise us to be on our guard always, since a little bit of caution could save us from a terrible headache or even worse. We were curious about what "worse" meant, but she would not tell us. We asked how to stay perpetually "on guard". She advised us to gear up with holy water and amulets. Nora related she was able to diagnose if someone had been given the evil eye by dropping olive oil into water. If the oil formed a starburst shape, the recipient had received the evil eye, or malocchio. She said she could offer help lift the curse but never wished to explain because she said the method for each person is different. I love that woman!

-Toni K.

My grandfather, Henry, was an architect in Manhattan back in the day. Since my grandmother, Nell, modeled in NYC, they would go in together quite a bit. Nell had become friends with people in the theater. Sometimes as she would wait for Henry to finish work, she would visit them before or after his/her shows. One day, prior to the beginning of the play, as my grandmother was about to leave backstage, one of the men was fooling around and shouted "Macbeth". That phrase is taboo in the theater. Supposedly, the play "Macbeth" is considered to be cursed and to utter that name before any performance is very bad luck. It can be said outside the theater, however. Anyway, this actor was told he needed to remove the curse immediately. So, although not thrilled this man who shouted "Macbeth" was required to leave the room, spin around three times, curse, knock, and ask permission to return.

In addition, my grandmother learned other superstitious theater traditions. A familiar one is to say "break a leg" instead of wishing another good luck. Another, is to bow at the end of the performance since it is good luck. Also, it is lucky for the theater staff to keep a light on when the theater was empty. I think that is a good idea anyway since no one wishes to trip over the many props and other items lying around. More fun tidbits which lead to bad luck for the actor include: not counting the people in the audience, do not leave personal items in the theater seats while rehearsing, don't whistle on or off stage, and when the announcement "five minutes" is called in order to come onto the stage, everyone needs to say a loud "thank you". Interesting! Now you know showbiz talk!

-Toni K.

A very long time ago, when I was a preteen, my best friend, Kathy, and I loved to hang out in the woods behind my parents' farm. We adored an adventure and every so often we'd find one. Each time we explored the woodlands, my father's German Shepard, Fritz, would accompany us. Fritz protected us and we felt safe the further and further we walked into the dense group of trees. This day, however, we did not have Fritz with us. He loved rides with my father and they were both out that afternoon together. Kathy and I were laughing so hard on our walk that day that we did not realize how far we had gotten. Plus, we were proud of ourselves since we felt brave without Fritz until, we reached a rather large body of water that we had never noticed before that time. We stopped in our tracks and noticed the sun was setting. Kathy remarked she wished we had Fritz along with us. I heartily agreed. All of a sudden, an elderly woman dressed in what appeared to be a black monk's robe, appeared. She looked disturbed that we were there. This woman motioned to the water and told us there was a full moon tonight. She added if we stayed with her until the moon appeared and reflected on the water, we would have ten years of good luck. Kathy and I quickly declined, ran back to my house and told my parents all about it. My father remarked he didn't recall a pond in that area or ever seeing an old lady. My mother NEVER heard of that particular superstition and she is a superstition expert. She forbade us to play in the woods ever again-with or without Fritz.

-Toni K.

Growing up with my Mom and grandmother in the same home, we heard a lot of sayings that I always felt were kind of strange. For instance, when we had overnight guests, I had to sleep in my Grandma's bedroom with her. She always use to tell me that the first person to fall asleep should whistle. That way we would know when the other was asleep.

Here are a few more:

- If we drove passed a hearse, my mother would always tell us to make a wish. (I always wished I would NOT be the next dead person riding in it!)
- And, if we drove passed a load of hay, we were also told to make a wish since it was for good luck.
- If we saw a ladybug in the house, my grandmother would take it outside and say "Ladybug, Ladybug fly away home, your house is on fire, your children will burn." (Maybe she thought it she didn't scare them into staying outside, we would have a ladybug infestation?)
- A bird flying into the house was considered bad luck.
- When you see a cardinal, it means a dead person is spirit visiting you.
- Death comes in threes. In my house any type of bad luck occurs three times in a relatively short amount of time.
- When one person dies, another person is born.
- Don't step on cracks, or you will break your momma's back.
- Don't cross your eyes because they will stay that way.
- A black cat crossing your path is bad luck.
- Don't walk under a ladder because it is bad luck.

-Beverly T.

Recently, I attended a funeral, and during the reception afterward, I was on the stairs making my way down from the second floor to the first. I noticed a woman standing at the bottom waiting for me. When I reached the bottom, she told me that it was bad luck to pass another person on the stairs. Then, she went on to share that it is bad luck to put a hat or shoes on the bed. I never expected a stranger to chat with me about her superstitions.

-Cortlee G.

We use to play a superstition game which now seems really silly. Here's how it works. If one person lights three different people's cigarettes with the same match, the third person in line will find out a baby is on the way. I remember one time, the third person was a guy. We would all just laugh, including the guy, and everyone knew what we were laughing about without saying anything to each other.

Another superstition my family followed was on New Year's Eve. We would all have to walk out the back door and then walk around the house and enter the front. Doing that would bring us luck all year long.

-Desiree B.

An Italian town (in Italy), always has a witch folk tale. When strange things start to occur, they blame the "town witch". Strange things started happening in my parents' house once my sister was born. My father started to see a black cat in their house. Since Italians are superstitious and believe in the "town witch", he believed she was entering his house as a cat. One night, he saw the cat, tried to shoo it away, and accidentally hit the cat with a broom handle on its back legs, to get it outside. The next morning, he was sitting on his front step ...the "town witch" passed by his house and she was limping! Was it a coincidence? Maybe yes, or no, but when you live in a small town everyone believes it.

-Giovanni M.

One day I was over my friend's house for a picnic. I was mentioning to his Dad's friend, Burt, that I had just seen the movie "Pet Sematary". Burt then told me the wildest story. Ten years ago, he got a black cat on a Friday the 13th and so he named him "Friday". Burt said the cat really wasn't that old when he found him dead on the porch one morning—or so he thought. Burt and his wife were very sad. They decided to bury Friday close to the house so they could visit his grave every day since they loved him so much. After one week, Friday returned to the house acting like nothing had ever happened. The grave was not disturbed. Friday returned on a Friday, but it was not on the 13th. Talk about a freaky Friday!

-Ian G.

As a kid I grew up with superstitions that I learned through my parents. Some I still believe in today, but some I have tried to break the "habit" of it being a bad thing.

- If a black cat crosses your path you will have bad luck.
- If you break a mirror you will have 7 years of bad luck.
- If you wash clothes on New Year's Day, you wash someone's life away.
- When people say "good luck" it's bad luck.
- Only pick up a penny if it is on heads or you will have bad luck.
- If you make a weird face and the moon changes, your face will stay like that.
- If you spill salt, you have to throw some over your shoulder or you will have bad luck.

- If you walk under a ladder, you will have bad luck.
- If your palm itches, depending if left or right, you will come into money or lose money.
- If your nose itches, you will get into a fight.
- If your ears ring, someone is talking about you.
- If you sneeze when someone is saying something or telling a story, then it's true.
- I would have to wear the same socks for a soccer game if we won and I was wearing them.
- A groom cannot see the bride in her dress before the wedding.
- Open an umbrella in the house – bad luck.
- If you say something and you're afraid of it happening, then you "knock on wood".
- Be careful on Friday the 13th because that day is bad luck.

-Jamie R.

When asked about any personal superstitions a couple of them come to mind immediately.

My mom came to the States from Scotland in 1949, hence her nickname, "Scotty".

Standing 4'10" Scotty was a powerful presence with a great sense of humor. She had a deep brogue that apparently everyone heard but me since I heard her speak all the time and never noticed. Except when she got mad and then I remember she rolled her r's alot.

I especially heard this brogue when I offended a superstition by ignoring the slings and arrows of the impending punishment and following through with the violation.

Two of these superstitions have a bit of a "theme". The first is, "No Shoes on the Table!" It makes sense, no one would want to place dirty shoes on the table, eeewwww. It was something that I would never ever do - so don't think I got yelled at a lot for this. No, not dirty shoes - clean shoes! Brand new shiny, leather smelling, crisp clean shoes that still had the tag on them and would be placed on the table to show off my bargain hunting.

Almost in slow motion my mother would reach across the table yelling, "noooooo, not on the table! It's bad luck!" She would admonish me as if I should know better and after so many years of hearing it I guess I should have. But each time I would immediately lift them high off the table (in the form of the "five second rule") in an attempt to undo the deed so it wouldn't count. Too late, here comes the lecture. Without any basis except "because I said so" I always countered with, "what, are the shoe gods going to get me if I put shoes on the table?" Now my mom was a very religious person, Catholic (so you can imagine her immediate conflict with my question). And referring back to her "powerful presence" it only took a look from her that said it all, don't you dare do it! Message received. Sorry, I asked. Won't happen again. Can I go?

It was the rebel in me that needed to get to the bottom of this restriction, not so much for understanding but more to support an opposing argument. Hence, the rebel part.

Research shows that the impending results of shoes on the table could negatively impact our financial outlook or even lead to an argument. (This further confused me because I was always told that an itchy nose would lead to an argument unless you kiss a fool - baaaa, geesch there's another one!)

Apparently, this legend comes from the mining industry. (Fun fact: The mining industry has been one of, if not, the most dangerous occupations with more injury and death rates than most other occupations). I preface this to emphasize the need for this superstition, as you are about to see. Families of the deceased miners would return home with the decedent's shoes and place them onto the table. My research did not explain why the table was the place of choice or what happened to the rest of the poor miner's belongs. Maybe it's part of a larger superstition. But clearly someone figured out that making it bad luck to place dirty shoes on a table where YOU EAT had to be stopped and back in the day offering bad luck would be the best deterrent. Today the best deterrent would be to threaten to take a picture and put it on social media.

The other superstition that plague me as a child was "no shoes on the bed". In an effort to save time the scenario with my mom was exactly the same as "no shoes on the table". Except that there is NO information to support that this is a real superstition. Shoes UNDER the bed, yes. But ON the bed, no.

Either way I don't recall any "bad luck" as a result of my negligence. However, I somehow feel betrayed and somewhat manipulated. But isn't that actually the intent of superstitions anyway?

-Jess P.

Both sets of my grandparents were born in Europe and emigrated to the U.S. in the early 1900's. My father's parents were from Hungary and my mother's parents were from Poland. Each brought their country's customs with them and passed them down through their families. I have many wonderful memories of the stories I heard and of the old country ways that I was taught.

My Hungarian grandmother was probably the most superstitious person in my family. Most of the superstitions she spoke of were related to food and grains to help keep farms and gardens productive. I remember one in particular. She told us crumbs on the tablecloth from Christmas dinner had to be fed to the chickens and the pigs to keep them healthy during the New Year. I guess that one would have been more important to us if we had had chickens and pigs. There are three other superstitions of hers that I will never forget.

Grandma told me that on the night of my wedding, I should put honey on my lips and my wife's lips just before our good night kiss so that our marriage would be long and sweet. Of course, that's exactly what I did.

My wife and I still do this on each anniversary. So far, there have been 15 of them.

Grandma also told me that I can trust the word of someone who sneezes during a conversation. She said it means whatever is being said is true. Never force a sneeze, though. It would bring bad luck.

The wildest thing Grandma said was a single woman should not sit at the corner of a table. If she did, she would never be married. I thought this was an odd thing to tell me and my brothers since we don't have any sisters. Maybe she had some insight into our futures. Each of us has at least one daughter now. None of us lets his daughter sit at the corner of a table.

The Polish side of my family had a few superstitions too. We were taught to never shake hands or hug in a doorway because it brings bad luck that ends your relationship with the person you greeted, that weddings which take place during a month the has the letter "r" in its Polish spelling will be blessed with good luck, and that counting pierogi while they cook will cause them to stick to the bottom of the pot or to be torn apart and lose their filling. I still live by them.

I didn't understand many of the superstitions I learned while growing up and I still don't understand them. This doesn't stop me from passing them to my children. It's simply a part of being in my family.

-Matt S

My Nan always told us that if a bird hits a window, it was a sign of death. Years ago, I was home with my Nan wrapping Christmas gifts when a bird hit our living room window. I remember being really scared and frightened because my Nan made the comment that she hoped it didn't mean she would be dying soon. The next day, she took sick and was taken by ambulance to the hospital, never to return home. She died on February 4, 1974. To this day, I believe that a bird hitting a window is a sign of death and have experienced this many times throughout my life.

-Pat R.

In the country I was born, Taiwan, the number four is bad luck. In Vietnam, it is the number three. Now that I live in the USA, I now know it is the number thirteen. We didn't care about the number thirteen there, but now that I'm here, I sure care!

Several Asian superstitions talk about prosperity. During the Chinese New Year, never borrow money because this means you will need to borrow money the entire year. Do not sweep your house during the first few days either since all your good luck may go straight out the door. And, do not say negative things at that time or you could jinx yourself.

-Rose Q.

To conclude, I have included a few quotes below by various personalities:

I'm a third time into a new book but sorry -I have a superstition about talking about it!
-Joanna Trollope

I have a superstition about saying too much about what I want to happen, just in case it disappears, or someone else comes along and beats me to it.
-Gil Gerard

Everyone has his superstitions. One of mine has always been when I started to go anywhere, or to do anything, never to turn back or stop until the thing intended was accomplished.
-Ulysses S. Grant

If there's a black cat that crosses the street in my path, I will turn around and walk 20 minutes out of my way to not cross it.
-Lauren Groff,

Evil eye jewelry must be a gift. You cannot buy it for yourself or it will not work.
-Giovanni M.

It was our pleasure to share these testimonials with you! I'm sure while reading these, you not only felt part of the story, but may have remembered a few of your own. What are your experiences with superstition?

The only superstition I have is that I must start a new book on the same day I finish the last one, even if it's just a few notes in a file. I dread not having work in progress.

—Terry Pratchett

THIRTEEN SONGS OF SUPERSTITION

You'll find superstition is a contagious thing. Some people let it get the better of them.

—Curt Siodmak

Numerous musical artists believe in the power of superstition and have written and/or sung tunes that reference the theme. It is nice to know we are not alone in our superstitious thinking.

In this section, I have selected thirteen songs by artists of different genres and time periods. My playlist includes singers who proclaim their good fortune and who sing melancholy melodies of bad luck.

Let's celebrate superstition with song. Below, I have provided partial lyrics for each song, plus my spin on the piece and/or a bit of history surrounding it. (If you'd like to read the complete lyrics, please consult https://www. azlyrics.com to search a particular song.)

I find it encouraging to see the weight the world of music places on superstition. I agree with the quote above by Curt Siodmak. Superstition is contagious!

Here are my thirteen picks in random order:

1. Superstition
2. Luck Be a Lady
3. Lucky
4. Good Luck, Bad Luck
5. With a Little Luck
6. A Good Run of Bad Luck
7. I Feel Lucky
8. Knock on Wood
9. Some Guys Have All the Luck
10. Black Cat
11. The Lucky One
12. Bad Luck
13. Thirteen

"Superstition"

Written and performed by Stevie Wonder

Stevie was only thirteen years old in 1963 when he had his first number-one hit. In 1972, he composed and recorded "Superstition," which mentions a few popular principles, such as mirrors, the number thirteen, and seven years of bad luck.

My analysis: Stevie Wonder tries to caution the listener about subscribing to superstition and its overall potential dangers.

> Very superstitious
> Writing's on the wall.
> Very superstitious
> Ladder's 'bout to fall.

Thirteen-month-old baby
Broke the looking glass.
Seven years of bad luck.

"Luck Be a Lady"
Written by Frank Loesser
Performed by Frank Sinatra

"Luck Be a Lady" was written in 1950. Prior to Frank Sinatra's rendition in 1960, it was sung by others and also was featured in the stage production of *Guys and Dolls*. "Luck Be a Lady" is one of my favorite Frank Sinatra songs.

My analysis: The lyrics of this catchy melody portray a man playing a game of chance while trying to maintain the interest of his lady love, who is becoming restless.

Luck be a lady tonight
Luck be a lady tonight
Luck if you've been a lady to begin with
Luck be a lady tonight
Luck let a gentleman see
Just how nice a dame you can be
I know the way you've treated other guys you've been with
Luck be a lady with me

"Lucky"
Written by Jason Mraz, Colbie Caillat, Timothy Fagan
Performed by Jason Mraz and Colbie Caillat

"Lucky" was released in 2000 and is a lovely pop duet. The gist of the song is that a person is very blessed if in love and committed to his or her best friend, who is that same person. They are fortunate (lucky) to have one another and look forward to seeing each other again when parted.

My analysis: I believe the thankfulness the two manifests their love for each other to a higher level. I especially enjoyed the scenery in this song's video.

> I'm lucky I'm in love with my best friend
> Lucky to have been where I have been
> Lucky to be coming home again
> Lucky we're in love in every way
> Lucky to have stayed where we have stayed
> Lucky to be coming home someday
> And so I'm sailing through the sea
> To an island where we'll meet

"Good Luck, Bad Luck"
Written by Ed King and Mike Estes
Performed by Lynyrd Skynyrd

Lynyrd Skynyrd, an American rock band that rose to fame in the 1970s, is known best for their Southern rock ballads, "Sweet Home Alabama" and "Free Bird." In 1994, "Good Luck, Bad Luck" appeared on their album, *Endangered Species.*

My analysis: I view this rock song as peppered with emotions about luck. The singer shares the story of his luck, both good and bad. Ultimately, the bad overpowers the good in his life, but he seems to take it in stride.

> I ain't the son of the seventh son, black cats won't cross my path
> Good luck comes I just watch it run and it sure does run out fast
> I wasn't born under no bad sign, but it was Friday the thirteenth

> Good luck—I'm the last to get it
> Bad luck—I'm the first

When it's good, ain't nothin' better
When it's bad, ain't nothin' worse
Good luck, bad luck

"With a Little Luck"
Written by Paul McCartney
Performed by Wings

Paul McCartney wrote "With a Little Luck" while at his farm in Scotland but later recorded it aboard a yacht in 1977. The entire song is five minutes and forty-five seconds in duration.

My analysis: This lively tune inspires the listener to have confidence that anything is possible if you believe in a bit of luck. I was hoping that the length of the song, 5:45, was a lucky number to the group and/or recording on the water was lucky.

And a little luck, we can clear it up
We can bring it in for a landing
With a little luck, we can turn it on
There can be no misunderstanding

With a little luck [x 2]
With a little luck, a little luck, a little luck
With a little luck [x 2]
With a little luck, a little luck, a little luck

"A Good Run of Bad Luck"
Written by Hayden Nicholas and Clint Black
Performed by Clint Black

This country song, released in 1994, rose to number one on the US charts. It was also featured on the movie soundtrack of *Maverick*.

My analysis: "A Good Run of Bad Luck" resembles a skewed version of "Luck Be a Lady," as gambling surrounds the love interest. The storyteller, a gambler, wishes to win the affection of his lady love. He equates winning and losing the game to their relationship and often uses the phrase, "Luck be a lady." Even though he has lost his money at the table due to a "run of bad luck," he is hopeful for a streak of good luck to follow.

To win her over, I'd seen the tables turn around
She's ten the hard way, I can feel it in my bones
She'll be makin' my day and not another night alone
'Til it's time for a windfall and not a single minute too soon
I've been too long overdue, now I'm gonna shoot the moon

I'd bet it all on a good run of bad luck
Seven come eleven and she could be mine
Luck be a lady, and I'm gonna find love comin' on the bottom line

"I Feel Lucky"
Written by Don Schlitz and Mary Chapin Carpenter
Performed by Mary Chapin Carpenter

"I Feel Lucky" is a country tune released in 1992.

My analysis: This high-spirited song tells of a woman who is positive she will win the current lottery, which totals eleven million dollars. She's so sure she will be a winner that she decides to buy a lottery ticket, skip work, and go to a local bar to celebrate her upcoming winnings in advance. In fact, she promises to buy her server a new car—a very generous offer, but I hope the bar employee did not take the hopeful winner seriously.

Well, I strolled down to the corner, gave my numbers to the clerk.
The pot's eleven million, so I called in sick to work.
I bought a pack of Camels, a burrito and a Barq's
crossed against the light made a beeline for the park.
The sky began to thunder, the wind began to moan.

I heard a voice above me sayin', "Girl, you'd better get back home."
I feel lucky,
I feel lucky, yeah.

"Knock on Wood"
Written by Eddie Floyd and Steve Cropper
Performed by Amii Stewart

"Knock on Wood" is a disco song recorded in the late 1970s, and at the time, it was one of my favorites. I remember riding in the car with my father, and this particular tune was blasting from the radio as he dropped me off at Catholic school. The nuns didn't appreciate it.

My analysis: This song depicts how certain folks feel about superstition. Some claim not to be superstitious but do not wish to take any chances. Amii sings she isn't superstitious but is not jeopardizing losing her love interest, so she will employ her lucky method and knock on wood.

I'm not superstitious about ya
But I can't take no chance
You got me spinnin', baby
You know I'm in a trance
'Cause your love is better
Than any love I know

The way you love me is frightening
You better knock, knock on wood, baby
Baby

"Some Guys Have All the Luck"
Written by Jeff Fortgang
Performed by Rod Stewart

Rod Stewart was not the first to sing "Some Guys Have All the Luck," but this rock song gave him a hit (and luck) in the 1980s.

My analysis: Rod sings about a lonely single guy who feels unlucky because his friends are all married. In addition, he envies seeing those who have significant others while he remains alone. It appears he has an ex-love, and the memory haunts him. This only adds to his being down on his luck.

Some guys have all the luck
Some guys have all the pain
Some guys get all the breaks
Some guys do nothing but complain
Woo woo woo

"Black Cat"
Written and performed by Janet Jackson

The title of this song suggests it's full of mystery and Halloween magic, but that is far from the truth. Even though Janet Jackson does make reference to a black cat with nine lives, this song is actually about gang life and violence.

My analysis: I think Janet is proving that she is superstitious on some level.

Black cat nine lives
Short days long nights
Livin' on the edge
Not afraid to die

But not for long
Better watch your step
Or you're gonna die

"The Lucky One"
Written and performed by Taylor Swift

Taylor Swift, an American musical artist, remains secretive about whom she is singing in "The Lucky One," but many have guessed it must be the musical icon Joni Mitchell.

My analysis: This melody tells of a celebrity who leaves behind the music industry to live a simpler, happier existence. One is left to ponder if Swift is alluding to the fact that she a "lucky one" too.

> New to town with a made up name in the Angel
> city, chasing fortune and fame
> And the camera flashes, make it look like a dream
> It was a few years later, I showed up here
> And they still tell the legend of how you disappeared,
> How you took the money and your dignity, and got the hell out
> But I think you got it right,
> Let me tell you now, you're the lucky one
> Let me tell you now, you're the lucky one, oh, oh, oh

"Bad Luck"
Written by Paul Rigby and Neko Case
Performed by Neko Case

"Bad Luck," released in 2018, is a poignant song. Neko Case was in Sweden, working on a new release, when she learned her house had burned down. After hearing the grim news, she went into the studio to record "Bad Luck," which she had written prior to the fire. Her lyrics took on a new meaning after the destruction of her home. She initially was sad about the news, of course, but later came to terms with the ordeal.

In Maggie Serota's article, "Neko Case—'Bad Luck'" (2018), she quotes Case as saying, "If somebody burned your house down on purpose, you'd feel so violated. But when nature burns your house down, you can't take it personally. In the big picture, my house burning was so unimportant. So many people lost so much more: lives and lives and lives." Case was referencing the destruction that had occurred in Puerto Rico, Texas, and in other parts of the United States.

My analysis: Neko Case is a believer in luck. I admire her fortitude, and I was moved by her statement. In the face of a personal horrific event, she embraced a very grateful attitude.

> Woke a dog from a running dream
> And that's bad luck (Bad luck)
> Ate a black fly in the cream
> And that's bad luck (Bad, bad luck)

> Could have stopped any one of these things
> But that would have been bad luck
> Are you tired of things going right?
> Things going wrong?

"Thirteen"
Written by Glenn Danzig
Performed by Johnny Cash

What better song to name as my thirteenth pick than "Thirteen"? Johnny Cash was a famous singer and songwriter, mostly recognized as a country singer. Cash also sang some gospel, blues, and folk songs. Although he did not pen "Thirteen," Cash delivers his usual heartfelt performance.

My analysis: This song depicts the narrator as a hellion who knows nothing but a life of misery. Thus, he brands the number thirteen on his neck. Way to go!

> Bad luck wind been blowin' at my back
> I was born to bring trouble to wherever I'm at
> Got the number thirteen tattooed on my neck

When the ink starts to itch
Then the black will turn to red
I was born in the soul of misery
Never had me a name
They just gave me the number

Listed below, in no particular order, are a few additional superstition-related titles. At your leisure, give them a listen.

- "No. 13 Baby"—Pixies
- "Unlucky"—The Shirelles
- "Broken Mirror"—Travis
- "Black Magic Woman"—Fleetwood Mac
- "Spit Three Times"—Neneh Cherry
- "Broken Mirrors"—Chromatics
- "Bloody Mary"—Lady Gaga
- "Good Luck Charm"—Jagged Edge
- "Good Luck Charm"—Elvis Presley
- "Bad Luck"—Social Distortion
- "You Got Lucky"—Tom Petty and the Heartbreakers

It was a blast selecting and examining thirteen songs for you. Musical artists take their heartfelt emotions and turn them into powerful and memorable tunes we enjoy for decades. What ideas entered your mind while reading the lyrics? Since writing this section, I have been motivated to pen my very own song.

The next time you walk under a ladder, break a mirror, or realize it is Friday the thirteenth, remember you're in good company.

What we don't understand we can make mean anything.

—Chuck Palahniuk

REFERENCES

AZLyrics. https://www.azlyrics.com.

Black, C., and H. Nicholas. 1994. "A Good Run of Bad Luck." https://www.lyricsfreak.com/c/clint+black/a+good+run+of+bad+luck_20032385.html.

BrainyQuotes. http://www.brainyquotes.com.

Burgess, Mitchell, and Robin Green. January 15, 2016. "Cursed." *Blue Bloods*. ABC television. https://www.imdb.com/title/tt5176120.

Calfas, Jennifer. 2017. "Here's How Much Meghan Markle's Engagement Ring Is Worth, According to Experts." *Money*. http://money.com/money/5037926/meghan-markle-prince-harry-engagement-ring.

Calliat, C., T. Fagan, and J. Mraz. 2000. "Lucky." https://www.azlyrics.com/lyrics/jasonmraz/lucky.html.

Carpenter, Mary Chapin, and D. Schlitz. 1992. "I Feel Lucky." https://www.azlyrics.com/lyrics/marychapincarpenter/ifeellucky.html.

Case, N., and P. Rigby. 2018. "Bad Luck." https://www.azlyrics.com/lyrics/nekocase/badluck.html.

Cropper, S. and E. Floyd. 1966. "Knock on Wood." https://www.google.com/search?source=hp&ei=OpJ1XLHUG-a_jwTLnZPAAg&q=lyrics+knock+on+wood+amii+stewart&oq=lyrics+knock+on+wood+by+amii&gs_l=psyab.1.0.0i22i30l3.80

7.11071..13444...1.0..0.250.4540.2j23j4......0....1..gws-wiz.....0..0j0i13
1j0i10j33i160.9EuqSDOvY78&safe=active.

Danzig, G. 1994. "Thirteen." https://www.azlyrics.com/lyrics/johnnycash/
thirteen.html.

Dark Shadows. 1966–1971. https://www.imdb.com/title/tt0059978.

De Paola, Maria. 2016. "Gender Differences in Superstition—Men Are
Influenced by Good Omens, Women by the Unlucky." https://digest.
bps.org.uk/2014/12/08/gender-differences-in-superstition-men-are-
influenced-by-good-omens-women-by-the-unlucky.

Escritos, Marcus. 2014. "10 Things That Sucked about Growing
Up a Jehovah's Witness." https://thoughtcatalog.com/marcus-
escritos/2014/08/10-things-that-sucked-about-growing-up-a-jehovahs-
witness.

Estes, M., and E. King. 1994. "Good Luck, Bad Luck." https://www.
azlyrics.com/lyrics/lynyrdskynyrd/goodluckbadluck.html.

Forbes Quotes: Thoughts on the Business of Life. http://forbes.com/quotes.

Fortgang, J. 1984. "Some Guys Have All the Luck." https://www.azlyrics.
com/lyrics/rodstewart/someguyshavealltheluck.html.

Fox, Martin. 2018. "How Many Dogs Are There in the World?" https://
www.quora.com/How-many-dogs-are-there-in-the-world.

Goodreads. http://www.goodreads.com.

Jackson, J. 1989. "Black Cat." https://www.azlyrics.com/lyrics/
janetjackson/blackcat.html.

Kerr, Mandy. 2019. "The Strange Superstitions of American Presidents,
Revealed." https://www.cheatsheet.com/culture/the-strange-
superstitions-of-american-presidents-revealed.html/HOME/
CULTURE.

Leonhardt, Mega. 2018. "Millennials Spend an Average of $3,000 on an Engagement Ring—Here's How to Get the Most for Your Money." https://www.cnbc.com/2018/08/07/millennials-spend-3000-dollars-on-a-engagement-ring.html.

Loesser, F. 1950. "Luck Be a Lady." https://www.azlyrics.com/lyrics/franksinatra/luckbealady.html.

McCartney, P. 1977. "With a Little Luck." https://www.azlyrics.com/lyrics/paulmccartney/withalittleluck.html.

Merriam-Webster Dictionary. "augury." https://www.merriam-webster.com/dictionary/augury.

Merriam-Webster Dictionary. "envy." https://www.merriam-webster.com/dictionary/envy.

Merriam-Webster Dictionary. "jealousy." https://www.merriam-webster.com/dictionary/jealousy.

Merriam-Webster Dictionary. "symbolism." https://www.merriam-webster.com/dictionary/symbolism.

Mitchell, Laura. 2018. "Is It Really Dangerous to Fly on Friday the 13th? The Truth Will Shock You." https://www.dailystar.co.uk/travel/travel-news/651855/Is-it-safe-to-fly-on-Friday-13th.

Moore, David W. 2000. "One in Four Americans Superstitious—Younger People More Superstitious than Older People." https://news.gallup.com/poll/2440/one-four-americans-superstitious.aspx.

National Vital Statistics System. Accessed, March 29, 2019. https://www.cdc.gov/nchs/nvss/deaths.htm.

Newsday.com. 2018. "Celebrities Born on Friday the 13th." https://www.newsday.com/entertainment/celebrities/celebrities-born-on-friday-the-13th-1.12951136.

Night Gallery. 1969–1973. https://www.imdb.com/title/tt0065327.

Oden, Bryant. 2011. "The Long Word Song." https://www.
google.com/search?source=hp&ei=MLZ2XK7aN4nr
Abe2oSwDw&q=the+long+word+song+worddrops.
com&btnK=Google+Search&oq=the+long+word+song+worddrops.
com&gs_l=psy-ab.3...1357.13286..13559...0.0..0.280.4388.5j
25j2......0....1..gws-wiz.....0..0j0i131j0i10j0i22i30j33i299j33i160.
ri3e6np_UvM&safe=active.

Pappas, Stephanie. 2015. "13 Freaky Things that Happened on Friday the
13th." https://www.livescience.com/49809-freaky-things-friday-the-
13th.html.

Paulos, John Allen. 2009. "Why Do We Believe That Catastrophes
Come in Threes? Recent Celebrity Deaths Highlight Our Fascination
with Threes." ABC News. https://abcnews.go.com/Technology/
WhosCounting/story?id=7988416&page=1.

Psycho. 1960. Alfred J Hitchcock Productions.

Ripma, Rob. 2015. "Top 5 Benefits of Bats." http://www.birdsandblooms.
com/blog/top-5-benefits-of-bats.

Romeo and Juliet: The Complete Play. 1993. http://shakespeare.mit.edu/
romeo_juliet/full.html.

Searing, Linda. 2018. "The Big Number: 3.8 Million Babies Were Born in
the U.S. Last Year. That's a Drop." https://www.washingtonpost.com/
national/health-science/the-big-number38-million-babies-were-born-
in-the-us-last-year-thats-a-drop/2018/05/25/ce96af5a-5f6f-11e8-a4a4-
c070ef53f315_story.html?noredirect=on&utm_term=.5bf6c8f4a959.

Serota, Maggie. 2018. "Neko Case—'Bad Luck.'" https://spin-music-
yahoopartner.tumblr.com/post/172806924935/neko-case-bad-luck.

Shafer, Lydia, and Sanger Shafer. 1987. "All My Exes Live in Texas." https://
www.azlyrics.com/lyrics/georgestrait/allmyexslivelintexas.html.

Statistics Portal. 2019. "Number of Married Couples in the United States from 1960 to 2018 (in Millions)." https://www.statista.com/ statistics/183663/number-of-married-couples-in-the-us.

Statistics Portal. 2018. "Number of Pets in the United States in 2017/2018, by Species (in Millions)." https://www.statista.com/statistics/198095/ pets-in-the-united-states-by-type-in-2008.

Statistics Portal. 2018. https://www.statista.com/statistics/198100/ dogs-in-the-united-states-since-2000.

Swift, T. 2012. "The Lucky One." https://www.azlyrics.com/lyrics/ taylorswift/theluckyone.html.

The Birds. 1963. Alfred J Hitchcock Productions.

"The Fascinating History of Elizabeth Taylor's Engagement Ring." 2018. https://www.estatediamondjewelry.com/history-elizabeth-taylors-ring.

The National Oceanic and Atmospheric Administration https:// oceanservice.noaa.gov/facts/sevenseas.html

The Seven Year Itch. 1955. 20th Century Fox.

The Sixth Sense. 1972. https://www.imdb.com/title/tt0068132.

Urban Dictionary. "Split the pole." https://www.urbandictionary.com/ define.php?term=Split%20Pole.

Weird News. 2017. "Black Cats Less Than Half as Likely to Be Adopted as Gray Cats." https://www.huffingtonpost.com/2013/10/21/black-cats-_ n_4137673.html.

Wonder, S. 1972. "Superstition."

https://www.azlyrics.com/lyrics/steviewonder/superstition.html.

Worldometers. https://www.worldometers.info.

Journal

Journal

Journal

Journal

Journal

I love this caricature. I'm holding a black cat and resemble
Samantha from the television show, *Bewitched*.

My grandmother Nell, holding my mother, Rowena.

My mother and my father, Joe. He wasn't superstitious, but humored us.

It can be a bit scary to flip the calendar page over to the 13th!

With my niece, Rowena, in wedding garb.

More wedding attire. My son, Ian, looking smashing
as he escorts my mother to her seat.

Bridal accessories.
My mannequin makes a beautiful bride. She is wearing
a traditional wedding veil, tiara, and pearls.

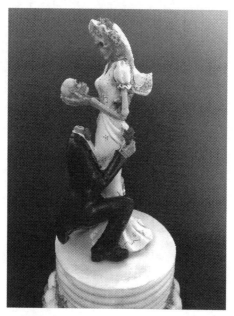

This is a unique wedding topper.

It is no longer customary to toss rice at the bride and groom as they exit the church. Bubbles are a fun alternative used to wish good luck.

Wedding Bands.
His band is very traditional, while mine is not.

Evil eye jewelry works best when it is received as a gift.

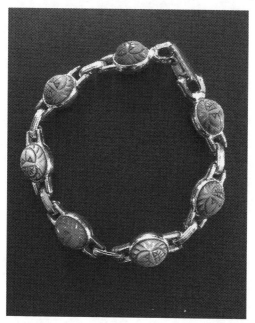

This bracelet features the image of a scarab beetle
carved into each stone. This is lucky!

Hamsa: This palm-shaped amulet is frequently used in jewelry designs and wall décor.

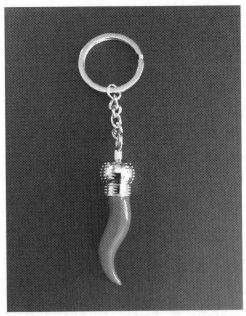

A cornicello, or horn, is a talisman worn to protect against the evil eye, and bad luck overall.

A rabbit's foot is considered a good luck token. In the olden
days, a lucky rabbit's foot was said to be the hind leg of a rabbit
which was killed in a cemetery, at night. I'm glad those days
are over. I am happy with my pink, synthetic version.

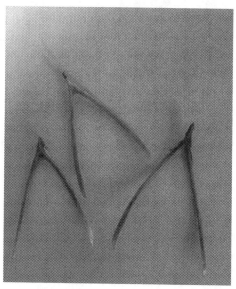

If you are the winner of a wishbone tugging contest, make
a wish. It is believed your wish will come true.

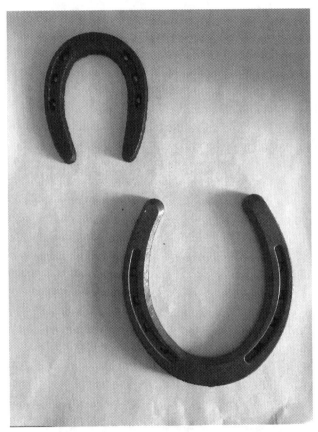

Is it your preference to place the points of the
horseshoe facing upward or downward?

Shoes on the table, whether in or out of the box, is a no-no. Unlucky!

Even though the reasoning pertaining to not opening an umbrella indoors is outdated, I still consider it to be a no-no.

Do not walk under a ladder which is forming the shape of a triangle (leaning against a wall or standing upright), for it is deemed unlucky. This ladder is one example.

A second example. This collapsible ladder forms a triangle as well. It is not advisable to walk underneath it.

I have often seen parked utility vehicles with a ladder hanging over its roof. I do not take any unnecessary chances, and stay far away, even though a triangle does not present itself in this scenario.

I work in a small city and notice a ladder here and there, which dangles over the sidewalk. Is it unlucky to walk beneath? Not technically, although you know my answer—walk around it. One day, after I snapped the picture of this ladder, I decided to conduct a brief study to see who walked under this ladder and who would avoid it. This study concluded, on that particular day, men walked directly under the ladder, yet women were cautious and chose to go around it.

My sweet rescue dog, "Little Bacca", who resembles
"Chewbacca", from the movie, *Star Wars*.

Ian, my son and lovable football player. He is very superstitious. Do you think he believes in superstition since I am his mother?

Printed in the United States
By Bookmasters